SERMON ON THE MOUNT

EXAMINING YOUR LIFESTYLE

PROJECT ENGINEER: Lyman Coleman, Serendipity House

WRITERS FOR NOTES: Richard Peace, William Cutler

WRITERS OF GROUP QUESTIONS: Andrew Sloan, Lyman Coleman, Denny Rydberg

COVER PHOTO: Robert Cushman Hayes.

TYPESETTING: Sharon Penington, Maurice Lydick, John Winson, Douglas LaBudde

PUBLISHER: Serendipity House is a resource community specializing in the equipping of pastors and church leaders for small group ministry in the local church in the English speaking world. A list of training events and resources can be obtained by writing to the address below.

SERENDIPITY GROUP BIBLE STUDY

Serendipity House / P.O.Box 1012 / Littleton, CO 80160

TOLL FREE 1-800-525-9563

95 96 97 98 99 /CH/ 6 5 4 3 2 1

Printed in the United States of America

Questions and Answers About

Starting a Bible Study Group

PURPOSE

1. *What is the purpose of a Bible study group?* Three things (and all three are important)

   a. Nurture—to be fed by God and grow in Christ, principally through Bible Study.

   b. Support—getting to know each other in a deeper way and caring for each other's needs.

   c. Mission—reaching out to non-churched people who are open to studying the Bible and reaching beyond your initial number until you can split into two groups . . . and keep multiplying.

NON-CHURCHED

2. *How can people who don't go to church be interested in studying the Bible?* Pretty easy. In a recent survey, the Gallup Poll discovered that 74% of the people in America are looking for a spiritual faith.

TURNED-OFF

3. *Then, why don't they go to church?* Because they have a problem with the institutional church.

SEEKERS

4. *What are you suggesting?* That you start a Bible study group for these kinds of people.

   - People who are turned off by the church but are looking for a spiritual faith.
   - People who are struggling with personal problems and need a support group.
   - People who are crippled by a bad experience with the church and want to start over in their spiritual pilgrimage.
   - People who are down on themselves and need encouragement to see beyond their own shortcomings.
   - People who are looking for hope in the face of seemingly insurmountable difficulties.
   - People who flashed across your mind as you read over this list.

RECRUITING

5. *How do I get started?* Make a list of the "honest seekers you know" and keep this list on your refrigerator until you have asked everyone.

FIRST MEETING

6. *What do we do at the first meeting?* Decide on your group covenant—a "contract" that spells out your expectations and rules (see the center section, page 3).

DEVELOPING A CONTRACT

7. *How do we develop a contract?* Discuss these questions and ask someone to write down what you agree upon (This "contract" will be used again at the close to evaluate your group).

   - What is the purpose of our group?
   - What are the specific goals?
   - How long are we going to meet? (We recommend 13 weeks. Then if you wish to continue, you can renew the contract).
   - Where are we going to meet?
   - What is going to be the starting and ending time at the sessions?
   - What about babysitting/refreshments, etc.?

LIFECYCLE

8. *How long should a Bible study group last?* This should be taken in stages. (See flow chart below)

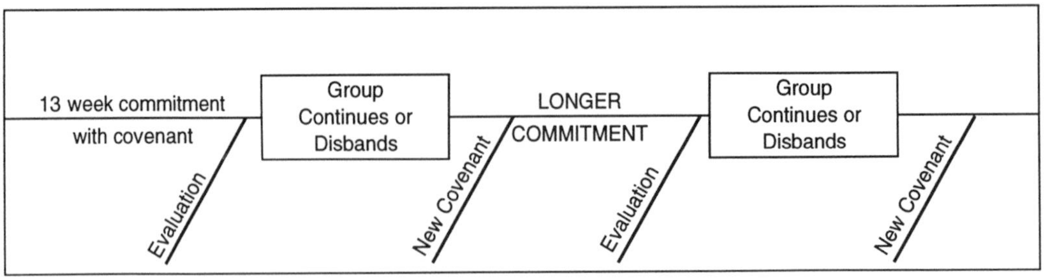

SHORT

9. *Why only a few weeks to start with?* Because people will give priority to something if they know it's not for long. And they can always renew and keep going if they wish.

STUDY PLANS

10. *How do we go about the study of this book of the Bible?* This should be decided at the first meeting. Inside the front cover is a suggested schedule that you can follow.

HOMEWORK

11. *Is there any homework?* No—unless you want to do some research about a particular concern. If you are studying one of the longer books of the Bible, where you do not have time to cover every passage, you may want to follow the "Reading" suggestions for this course of study.

BIBLE IGNORANCE

12. *What if we have people in the group who know nothing about the Bible?* Great. This is what this group is all about. There are NOTES on the opposite page to refer to if you have any questions about a word, historical fact or significant person in the passage.

NOTES

13. *Who wrote these Notes?* Richard Peace, a Professor at Gordon Conwell Seminary and a recognized Bible scholar.

SERENDIPITY

14. *What is Serendipity?* A small research foundation that specializes in programs for support groups in a Christian context.

DREAM

15. *What is your dream?* Christian support groups for hurting and struggling people inside and outside of the church—built around a study of Scripture and care for one another. For further information, we invite you to call:

TOLL FREE 1-800-525-9563, IN COLORADO 303-798-1313.

Introduction to

THE SERMON ON THE MOUNT

Well Known...But Neglected

The Sermon on the Mount, like the Ten Commandments, is one of the best-known passages in the Bible. Many people are at least somewhat familiar with the Beatitudes, the Lord's Prayer, the admonition to "consider the lilies of the field," and the parable of the two men who built their houses on sand and on rock.

Yet the Sermon on the Mount is undoubtedly much better known than it is understood or practiced! Often a person will casually remark, "Well, I think all we have to do is live by the teachings in the Sermon on the Mount and we'll be okay with God." Such an offhand statement that assumes the Sermon is merely a rehash of basic moral principles which "good" people follow anyway betrays a lack of understanding of the Sermon's call for a deep, inner righteousness that "surpasses that of the Pharisees and teachers of the law" (Mt 5:20). There is far more than common moral maxims here!

Other people assume the Sermon on the Mount has nothing to do with the way a Christian lives today. They believe the Sermon only applies to a future age, and see the Sermon's teachings (which seemingly stress human effort over God's grace) as having no relevance for the church. But much of what is found in the Sermon on the Mount is also found elsewhere in the teachings of Jesus and Paul. One would have to dismiss the relevancy of much of the New Testament to evade the force of this Sermon!

A third view assumes the Sermon is meant to accomplish exactly the opposite of what the proponents of the first view assert! Rather than giving us a basic moral program to follow, this view teaches that the Sermon is meant to break us of any hope that we can live by the laws of God. It is meant to drive us to God for mercy and grace as we realize we cannot live up to God's stringent demands. Once we have recognized this, the Sermon has done its job as the new law that leaves us broken before God, finally able to receive God's grace. The difficulty of this view is that it provides the Christian with no direction as to how one is actually supposed to live. What does God call us to be and do once we recognize our brokenness?

A fourth view takes the Sermon very seriously as the law of the kingdom of God as laid down by Jesus. Its teachings (or at least those sections that do not require self-mutilation!) are to be applied literally. Thus, oaths are forbidden. Divorce is permitted only for adultery. Remarriage is prohibited. The use of force is never an option. Pledging to church budgets is rejected. The difficulty with this view is that the "law" of Jesus ends up becoming far more harsh and impersonal than that of Moses. It ends up leading a person to take a legalistic approach to the very words of Jesus that were in large part directed at exposing the folly of the legalistic approach of the Pharisees!

The Sermon on the Mount is not a stringing together of moral precepts that provide good advice on how to live, nor is it a picture of life in some far off "kingdom age" that has no relevance for the church, nor is it meant simply to crush its readers into despair, nor is it a new legal code to be enforced by the church. *Rather, the Sermon on the Mount is a picture of what the inner character of the follower of Jesus in any age should be like.* In this Sermon, people come face to face with the radical demands of the Kingdom of God brought near by the coming of Jesus. This is the manifesto of God's Kingdom which "describes what human life and human community look like when they come under the gracious rule of God."[1] In this brief sermon, Matthew presents the reader with unforgettable pictures of what it means to be a follower of Jesus.

Background to the Sermon

It is commonly thought that the gospels are biographies of Jesus, a record of the day-to-day activities of Jesus written down by authors who functioned like a modern reporter recording "just the facts." Such a view is inadequate. A closer examination of the gospels reveals that the authors were more like editors than reporters. Using an analogy from television, they are the producers, not the camera crew; they are not simply aiming the camera at whatever action happens to be going on, but are cutting and splicing the film to create an effect. The authors of the gospels took the stories and sayings of

Jesus and presented them in various ways in order to accent various truths about Jesus' identity, his mission, and his call to discipleship.

It is important to note in this regard that the Sermon is given primarily to Jesus' disciples (5:1). The crowds are present (5:1; 7:28), but the immediate audience is those who professed allegiance to Jesus. *The Sermon is not the program one must follow in order to **become** a disciple, but is the way of life that is to be pursued by those who **are** disciples.* Like all the biblical writers, Matthew makes it clear that a relationship with God is a gift one receives by God's grace: Jesus is the light to all nations, calling upon people to receive the kingdom of God (4:17). He graciously invites people to become his disciples (4:18–22). He reaches out in love to all who call upon him in faith (8:2–3,5–7; 9:2,22,29). No one earns his way to God (19:16ff.), and no one is so indebted to God that he or she is without hope (18:21–35). Salvation is a gift of God.

Those who receive the gift, however, are expected to reflect the presence of the kingdom in their lives. The Sermon on the Mount reveals what that should look like in terms of a person's attitudes and actions. It shows the reader the lifestyle God desires to develop in the community of people who are following Jesus. It sets the standard for which Christians are to reach in their attitudes and relationships. It is a high goal meant to reveal the mediocrity with which most of us are comfortable and to stir us to action. Here we have a picture of personal and social righteousness that refuses to be limited. The teachings in the Sermon are the practical outworking of God's call for his people to love God and neighbor. The lifestyle embraced in this Sermon is the goal pursued by those who have been motivated and empowered by God's grace.

The Focus of the Sermon

A very rough outline of the Sermon on the Mount would be to divide it into three sections:

5:1–20 The Character of the Disciple
5:21–7:6 Examples of This Character
7:7–27 Admonitions to Pursue This Character

While such a division is obviously simplistic, it focuses our attention on the central issue of the Sermon, which is the character of the follower of Jesus. Matthew 5:20 underscores the point: the Sermon exposes the need for a righteousness which exceeds that of the scribes and Pharisees. This is not meant to belittle the Pharisees, as if they were hypocritically pretending to be something they knew perfectly well they weren't. The Pharisees *were* deeply concerned about being righteous, if one considers righteousness to be a matter of outwardly conforming to the regulations, laws, and traditions which they valued.

For instance, one sect of Pharisees were known as the "Bruised and Bleeding Pharisees." These men were so concerned about holiness that they took extreme measures to protect themselves from sin. In order to avoid thoughts of lust, for example, they would blindfold themselves when out in public to avoid having to look at women! The resultant problem of bumping into things and falling led to their nickname! They were very much concerned with being righteous, but Jesus pointed out that their approach was inadequate. Although it seemed to be an extreme response to the problem of lust, it was not extreme enough! His call for people to gouge out an eye and throw it away if it led them to sin may be an intentional commentary on the ineffectiveness of the way the Bruised and Bleeding Pharisees dealt with the problem of lust. Simply closing one's eyes was not sufficient; a more radical approach was needed that would get to the heart-attitude involved.

The Sermon on the Mount is not meant to be a "new law" in the sense that Jesus was laying down new regulations for people to observe. People then (and now) did not need more rules to tell them how God wanted them to live. There were plenty of perfectly good rules already. The problem, as illustrated by the history of Israel, was that people consistently minimized or bent the rules in order to fit their interests. It was this approach to God's law that allowed the Pharisees to assume, for instance, that since they had not actually murdered anyone they had therefore fully kept the sixth commandment. It was this approach that allowed them to assume that if a divorce could be legal, then it must be moral.

This literalistic, legalistic approach to the law was what Jesus exposed, challenged, and reformed. He had no new law to give, but called for a new heart. His concern was that his followers should have their character shaped and formed by the character of God.

Interpreting the Sermon

The variety of views about the Sermon as well as its nature as a collection of sayings makes the question of how to interpret specific passages a difficult one. In addition, there are other considerations that affect interpretation.

For example, the Sermon is full of images and customs that need to be understood in the light of Jesus' culture. Disciples are "the light of the world." They are not to "give dogs what is sacred." They are to "enter through the narrow gate," and to "turn the other cheek" when struck on one side. Proper application of these teachings requires a sense of what that image or custom meant in Jesus' day. For example, most North Americans today only use salt as a flavoring for food, but in Jesus' day it was also used as the means of preserving food from spoiling. That gives a different twist to the picture of Jesus' disciples as "the salt of the earth." Likewise, a new perspective on the command to turn the other cheek is gained when it is understood that this refers to the disciple's response to what was an insulting gesture, not a physical assault. The notes that accompany these studies attempt to provide this background.

A second consideration affecting interpretation is familiarity with the rabbinic style of teaching. Often, a rabbi would state a general principle and then provide "case studies" to illustrate his point. While the principle was meant to be understood as a universal maxim, its application to a particular situation was not a simple matter. It was up to the rabbi to make the application. Jesus himself employed this teaching style. For instance, in 5:39a, he asserts the principle of non-retaliation and then, in verses 39b–42, gives four case studies that illustrate the principle.

A third factor that deeply affects interpretation is the issue of which teachings are meant to be understood literally and which are to be understood figuratively. Hyperbole, a common manner of speaking in Jesus' culture, uses exaggeration to grab attention and make a point. It makes an extreme, absolute statement but is never intended to be actually interpreted and applied absolutely. Rather, it is meant to demonstrate a strong contrast with prevailing opinion so that one's mind is forced to consider a new way of thinking about a matter.

Scholars agree that hyperbole is used in this Sermon, but they disagree strongly about where and when it is used. Most people would agree that hyperbole is involved in the command to "not let your left hand know what your right hand is doing" (6:3) when one gives to the needy. This statement, which obviously could not be followed literally, is seen as a strong rebuke to the ostentatious display of almsgiving practiced by the Pharisees. However, Christians are deeply divided about whether the statements "anyone who marries the divorced woman commits adultery" (5:32) or "do not resist an evil person" (5:39) are to be understood hyperbolically or literally. Many churches interpret and apply the former command literally, prohibiting divorce and remarriage, but understand the latter figuratively, allowing their members to participate in wars against aggression. The reasons for how such decisions are made are not always clear.

There are four helpful guidelines to keep in mind in trying to discern whether or not a statement is hyperbolic:

(1) *What is the context to which Jesus is speaking?* Much of the Sermon on the Mount is a sharp contrast to the traditions and practices of the Pharisees and scribes (5:20, 21, 27, 31, 33, 38, 43; 6:2, 5, 16), which ended up justifying actions and attitudes that were deeply sinful. In those cases, it is helpful to know some of the background of the traditional practices regarding divorce, oath-taking, almsgiving, prayer, etc. to which Jesus is presenting an alternative. The questions then become: "What are the specific abuses he is seeking to correct?" and "In what similar ways are those abuses present today?"

(2) *If a person practiced this command literally, would that really deal with the inner issues involved?* Throughout the Sermon, Jesus is exposing the folly of considering righteousness as a matter of outwardly conforming to the law and traditions. His focus is on the inner attitudes involved. Cutting out my eye will leave me blind, but will not touch my heart that lusts after what my eye has seen. Something far more radical is demanded if the root problem of sin is to be dealt with. While I may obey the admonition in 5:34 to "not swear at all" and thus refuse to take oaths, the real issue is whether or not I am a person whose word can be trusted. That, and not the external matter of whether or not one takes an oath in court, is Jesus' point here.

(3) *Does the literal practice of this command square with other teachings of the Bible on the subject?* In the Sermon, Jesus is really reiterating the essence of the Old Testament call for God's people to be holy. The rest of the New Testament likewise reinforces this call. There is nothing essentially unique in the Sermon regarding the ethics or morals of the Christian life. Therefore, the rest of Scripture provides "checks and balances" on our interpretations. The call to pray in one's room with the door closed (6:6) needs to be interpreted in light of the gathered prayer of the church (seen in Acts 4:24 and in many other places).

(4) *Does the literal application of this teaching square with the general ethical tenor of the Bible that puts a stress on human wholeness, love, and justice?* In the Sermon, Jesus clearly stands against any form of righteousness that seeks to measure itself by external conformity to some law. His concern is with the attitudes of the heart that motivate our behavior. In spite of the literal command of 5:39, in some cases it might be more loving and just for people to stand against an evil person than to allow him or her to harm many others. The admonition here is meant to challenge people to replace their inner desire for vengeance against those who oppose them with the better way of loving service. It is not a denial of the need and appropriateness for systems of social justice such as the courts.

The Challenge of the Sermon

All of these considerations indicate that a study of the Sermon on the Mount is a challenging task! It will stretch us intellectually and spiritually. We will be tempted at times to minimize some of the hard teachings. Sometimes we will think we have found an escape hatch by saying that a certain teaching is hyperbolic, only to find that the reality exposed by that hyperbole is far more challenging than simply conforming to the statement itself. John W. Miller, in his brief but profound study on this Sermon, writes:

You who take up this study, having enlisted in this movement (of the kingdom of God) at this time, should pause at this point to reflect on your readiness. Perhaps in considering Christianity you had in mind simply joining a "church." You may not have thought of the church as a "movement" calling for radical changes in your life. Or you may have thought that Christianity was primarily a matter of believing certain dogmas. You did not realize that it is far more a call to action, a call to discipleship and sometimes hard obedience. Perhaps you thought that your main responsibility as a Christian would be to go to worship services on Sunday and live a respectable life. You did not realize that joining up would involve you in a whole new life-style, one that might well bring you into opposition to the "kingdoms of this world." Consider: Do you want to leave the crowd and join the disciples who follow Jesus in this radical way?2

1 John Stott, *The Message of the Sermon on the Mount*, InterVarsity Press, p. 18.
2 John W. Miller, *The Christian Way*, Herald Press, 1969, p. 21.

UNIT 1—Introduction / Matthew 5:1–5

Scripture

The Beatitudes

5 ***Now when he saw the crowds, he went***
up on a mountainside and sat down. His
disciples came to him, [2]and he began to
teach them, saying:

[3]"Blessed are the poor in spirit,
for theirs is the kingdom of heaven.
[4]Blessed are those who mourn,
for they will be comforted.
[5]Blessed are the meek,
for they will inherit the earth.

Group Questions

Every group meeting has three parts: **(1) To Begin** (15 minutes) to break the ice; **(2) Read Scripture and Discuss** (30 Minutes); and **(3) To Close and Pray** (15-30 Minutes). Try to keep on schedule. The most important time is the prayer time.

TO BEGIN / 15 Minutes (Choose 1 or 2)

- ❑ What is the tallest mountain in your state?
- ❑ Where would you go if you wanted to take your friends for a retreat?
- ❑ What do you do when you want to get away from crowds of people?

READ SCRIPTURE AND DISCUSS / 30 Minutes

- ❑ When did you first get interested in Bible study?
- ❑ Who is someone you look to for spiritual teaching?
- ❑ How do you define "poor in spirit"? What do you consider to be its opposite?
- ❑ Given the choice between "the kingdom of heaven" and winning the lottery, which would you choose? Why?
- ❑ Growing up, what was the attitude in your home toward sharing emotions like crying?
- ❑ Are you more open with your emotions now or when you were a child?
- ❑ Who do you admire as a good example of meekness?
- ❑ As you begin studying the Beatitudes, how would you describe your attitude right now?

TO CLOSE AND PRAY / 15-30 Minutes

- ❑ What motivated you to sign up for this Bible study course?
- ❑ What would you like to see happen in this Bible study group?
- ❑ Who would you like to invite next week to the meeting?
- ❑ How can this group remember you in prayer this week?

Notes

Summary. The so-called Sermon on the Mount is the first (and longest) of five major teaching sections in Matthew. Here, Jesus focuses on the subject of the kingdom of heaven and what is involved in living as a part of it. The Sermon on the Mount is not merely a collection of general ethical principles (though it does present a profound ethic); it is a focused reflection on what is involved in living in obedience to God. This is not the only place where Jesus raises these matters. Portions of his teachings can be found elsewhere in the Gospels.

5:1–2 *a mountainside.* Literally, "the mountain." It is not the topography but the theology that is important here. To the original Jewish readers, this would have been an inescapable allusion to the time long ago when Moses climbed Mt. Sinai and delivered the Law to Israel. Jesus is being portrayed as the "one like" Moses to whom the people are to listen (Dt 18:15).

sat down. Typically, when rabbis taught in the synagogue, they would sit rather than stand (like modern preachers). This also accents Jesus' authoritative position.

disciples. This teaching is for everyone who would be a follower of Jesus.

5:3-10 The "Beatitudes" are so named because in the Latin translation each of the eight statements begins with the word *"beatus."* Such pronouncements of blessedness were common in the OT, particularly the Psalms (see Ps 1:1; 32:1-2). Each of Jesus' beatitudes begins by defining the character (the spiritual state) of those who are members of the kingdom of God; it then moves to the reward such a person can expect. For all but the first and last beatitudes, the rewards are each expressed in the future tense. However, the Beatitudes have both a present and a future fulfillment. The Beatitudes are not defining eight different types of people but the characteristics that are to be found in every child of God. While there is a tension in this section (and throughout the Sermon on the Mount) between the ideal (presented here) and the real (the presence of sin and failure), Jesus is here defining the character that is to be formed in his disciples.

5:3 *Blessed are.* The Greek word *makarios* refers to those who are to be congratulated or who are fortunate or well off. It does not mean they are happy or prospering. Instead, whether or not they know or feel it, they are fortunate because their condition reflects that they are in a right relationship to God. In commenting on the meaning of this word as it is found in the beatitudes of the Psalms, Martin Buber wrote, "This is a joyful cry and an enthusiastic declaration: How fortunate indeed is this man! In the cry, timeless by its nature, the division of now and later, of earthly and future life is virtually absorbed... The psalmist obviously wishes to say, 'Pay attention, for there is a secret good fortune... which counterbalances and outbalances all misfortune. You do not see it, but it is the true, indeed the only good fortune'" (Lapide).

poor in spirit. This phrase does not refer to those who are poor in the material sense, but to those who acknowledge their need of God. Luke's version omits the words "in spirit." Quite often, both in the OT and the NT, the spiritually poor were literally poor as well, because their insistence on being faithful to God made them targets of oppression and exploitation by those who compromised God's standards for their own material gain. For instance, Isaiah 61:1ff., which serves as a background for the Beatitudes, announces the coming of God's deliverance to the Jewish exiles who were "lowly" (poor), "brokenhearted" (mourning), and "captives" in a hostile land (the meek). These are the people who live in humble dependence on God (see Ps 34:6). It is not an idealistic notion of the supposed simplicity of poverty, but rather a reflection of the inner character of the person who would be a follower of Jesus. "... a proper understanding of (this Sermon) requires a divine transformation of the human spirit ... it cannot be read properly apart from an acknowledgment of our spiritual bankruptcy ... an acknowledgment of our poverty and of our need to be transformed is the first condition that the Sermon on the Mount imposes" (Vaught).

theirs is the kingdom of heaven. This pronouncement ushers in a new order. Traditionally, Jews assumed the reign of God meant the exaltation and leadership of Israel over all the nations. In one brief sentence, Jesus undermines such nationalistic ideas. God's kingdom, conceived of as a state of peace, fullness, justice, and abundance (Is 42; 49; 51; 65:17–25), is promised to *anyone* recognizing his or her need for God. Whether or not one was an Israelite was simply no longer the defining issue! The Beatitudes assert that in Jesus this deliverance has come for *all* types of people who acknowledge their need and dependence upon God. Such is Jesus' message to any group who would assume that only certified members of that particular religious, racial, or ethnic group are heirs to God's kingdom.

5:4 *those who mourn.* This does not refer to those bereaved by the common tragedies that come upon all people, but to those who are in touch with the pain of the world caused by the pride, arrogance, and evil of people who do not recognize their bankruptcy before God. In short, this is a mourning over sin, both that which is intensely personal and that which is broadly social. These are people who mourn over their own sin and its consequences to others. These are people who mourn over the way sin infects even the best-intentioned social, governmental, and religious structures, and often leads these systems to inflict harm on multitudes of people. These are people who mourn over the pain that has come to them, because their commitment to follow the way of the kingdom of God has been met by hostility and ridicule from others. These are people who mourn over the pain that human evil brings to the whole world.

they will be comforted. "(Christian spirituality) ... demands that we own our personal brokenness, especially that which occurs because of our own sin. It demands that we confess that we have betrayed our call to be faithful to God's plan. If we do not admit that sin is part of our experience and mourn over it we will be controlled by it. But, to the depth and degree that we own the brokenness in our individual lives, to the same depth and degree we will experience the blessedness of God's comfort, healing, and consolation. Only when we are willing to face our own inner alienation from God will we be able to experience the sense of wholeness that expresses messianic peace and fulfillment" (Crosby).

5:5 *the meek.* This is similar in meaning to the phrase "the poor in spirit." It involves a lifestyle marked by gentleness, humility, and courteousness. The word used here for meekness is the same one used of Jesus himself in Matthew 11:28–30 in which he is called "gentle and humble in heart."

they will inherit the earth. The irony of God's reign is that, despite the efforts of those who grasp for the world, it will one day be given over to those who have demonstrated a life of meekness. This was dramatically seen in two instances in Israel's past, e.g., in the Exodus from Egypt and, centuries later, when Israel was restored to Palestine after the Exile in Babylon. The mightiest nations on earth (first Egypt, and then Babylon) could not prevent God from accomplishing his plan for his people.

On Poverty of Spirit . . .

This is not simply an internal attitude of feeling bad about myself. That is simply having low self-esteem. The attitude called for here is illustrated by Jesus' call to the rich young ruler. Only as he sold all that he had (and thus gave up the props which allowed him to maintain his illusion that he had somehow earned such blessings from God) and gave it away to help others could he be a true follower of Jesus. "The reign of God is composed of people who (sell) their power, possessions, and prestige in such a manner that they enable conditions of powerlessness, poverty, and depression in others to be alleviated" (Michael Crosby, *Spirituality of the Beatitudes,* Orbis, 1981, p. 49).

On mourning . . .

"When was the last time we really grieved over such things as the sexism in our churches, the consumerism that tears apart families, or the ideology that justifies destruction of whole peoples and environment in the name of freedom? Healing will never come (within our society) until we first admit the existence of the sins and cultural addictions that contribute to human and societal brokenness, and then mourn over them" (Michael Crosby, *Spirituality of the Beatitudes,* Orbis, 1981, p. 90).

On meekness . . .

As can be seen from the life of Jesus, meekness means neither weakness nor timidity. Rather, it means a compassionate use of one's strengths for the good of others. Philippians 2:4–7 provides an illustration of this quality in that Jesus willingly laid aside his rights as the divine Son of God in order to give himself in service to humanity. In that letter, Paul holds out the example of Jesus as a model for all Christians to imitate. "The aggressive (people) are unable to enjoy their ill-gotten gains. Only the meek have the capacity to enjoy in life all those things that provide genuine and lasting satisfaction" (Robert Mounce, *Matthew: A Good News Commentary,* Harper and Row, 1985).

UNIT 2—The Beatitudes / Matthew 5:6–12

Scripture

6 Blessed are those who hunger and
thirst for righteousness,
for they will be filled.
7 Blessed are the merciful,
for they will be shown mercy.
8 Blessed are the pure in heart,
for they will see God.
9 Blessed are the peacemakers,
for they will be called sons of God.
10 Blessed are those who are persecuted
because of righteousness,
for theirs is the kingdom of heaven.

11 "Blessed are you when people insult you,
persecute you and falsely say all kinds of evil
against you because of me. 12 Rejoice and be
glad, because great is your reward in heaven,
for in the same way they persecuted the
prophets who were before you.

Group Questions

Every group meeting has three parts: **(1) To Begin** (15 minutes) to break the ice; **(2) Read Scripture and Discuss** (30 Minutes); and **(3) To Close and Pray** (15-30 Minutes). Try to keep on schedule. The most important time is the prayer time.

TO BEGIN / 15 Minutes (Choose 1 or 2)

- ❑ What was your favorite thing to eat or drink when you were a kid?
- ❑ What teacher, coach or other person taught you a lot about attitude and character?
- ❑ Who in your family would you nominate for a Nobel Peace Prize because of their peace-making ability?

READ SCRIPTURE AND DISCUSS / 30 Minutes

- ❑ Are the Beatitudes applicable to life today, or better applied to the lives of Jesus' audience?
- ❑ If a political party was to make the Beatitudes their platform, what would happen to that party on election day?
- ❑ What is the hungriest or thirtiest you've ever been: Physically? Spiritually?
- ❑ Are you better at showing mercy or receiving mercy?
- ❑ If gold is purified by fire, what purifies the heart?
- ❑ What means is used to "make peace" in your home? At work? In your church?
- ❑ Who do you admire for taking a stand, especially in the face of opposition?
- ❑ Which of the Beatitudes are you strongest in? Weakest in?

TO CLOSE AND PRAY / 15-30 Minutes

- ❑ How do you feel about this Bible study? About your Bible study group?
- ❑ If you could change one thing about this study or group, what would it be?
- ❑ Did you invite someone new this week?
- ❑ How can this group help you in prayer this week?

Notes

5:6 *hunger and thirst for righteousness.* Kingdom people are not to be stuck in the mourning of their sin and spiritual poverty, but are to be stirred by such insight into positive action that marks their conversion to a whole different way of life. In the ancient world, hunger and thirst were common experiences. Hungry and thirsty people have only one passion. Their entire energy is focused upon finding food and water. They will lay aside other pursuits in order to get these critical needs met. Likewise, people in Christ's kingdom are marked by this same deep-seated, intense need and longing for knowing and living in God's way (see Ps 42:1–2; Isa 55:1–2). Righteousness is not so much a matter of living in compliance with a set of laws as it is living in such a way that reflects the character of God in all of one's relationships. "... the desire for righteousness ... means ultimately the desire to be free from sin in all its forms and in its every manifestation" (Lloyd-Jones). Stated positively, it is a desire to pursue God's will in every aspect of one's life (see also Mt 6:33). It is the human action associated with the request in the Lord's Prayer for God's will to "be done on earth as it is in heaven."

filled. Because righteousness defines the very character of God, those who pursue it can be assured of the ultimate satisfaction of their desire when God's kingdom is manifested in all its fullness.

5:7 *the merciful.* Just as righteousness is part of the very nature of God, so is mercy. To be merciful is not a matter of having an easygoing nature that simply lets a lot of things go by, but it is an act of deliberate compassion and kindness toward those who do not deserve it. The OT Law instituted mercy through the provision of the Year of Jubilee, during which all slaves were to be freed, all debts cancelled, and all land returned to the original owners (Lev 25:8-55). It is this time of restoration that was used as a picture for what "the year of the LORD's favor" (Is 61:2) would be like for people enslaved and/or victimized by sin. Mercy focuses upon the pain, brokenness, and misery that marks the human condition as a result of sin and seeks to do what it can to relieve such conditions. Mercy gives freely to those to whom one is not expected to give at all. It offers forgiveness to those who have harmed us. It provides for the needs of those to whom we have no formal obligation. The motivation for such action stems from a person's recognition of his or her own spiritual bankruptcy; having seen the true condition of his or her own heart before God, he or she cannot help but extend mercy to others who are likewise bankrupt.

shown mercy. As the parable in Matthew 18 indicates, God's judgment of us reflects the way we treat others. This does not mean we earn God's mercy by our actions, but simply that those who refuse to show mercy betray that they have failed to recognize their own desperate need for God's mercy. In contrast, those who show mercy reveal that they recognize their own need for mercy. In this promise, Jesus assures them that they will indeed find mercy from God.

5:8 ***pure in heart.*** All of the Beatitudes have their roots in the ethic of the OT, including this one. "In Psalm 24:3ff access to God's presence during temple worship is for (the person) who has 'clean hands and a pure heart.' These are the spiritually 'pure,' not the ritually or ceremonially clean" (Hill). In the Bible, the "heart" is a shorthand way of referring to the whole personality, including the intellect, emotions, and actions. The call is for a thorough-going purity wherein every facet of our being is oriented toward a single-minded pursuit of God's way.

see God. In the OT, this term was used to describe someone who experienced the favor of God. The single-minded will know what no one yet has known: the full presence of God (see Jn 1:18 and Rev 22:4).

5:9 ***peacemakers.*** This beatitude calls for an active involvement in bringing about reconciliation between those in conflict, whether at the societal or personal level (see Ps 34:14). Peacemaking is neither a matter of minimizing conflict nor of using force to suppress hostilities. True peacemaking involves seeking heart-to-heart reconciliation between people. It requires the rooting out of the causes of alienation and the disciplined practice of attitudes and actions that truly work for harmony to take their place. The price of peacemaking is perhaps most solemnly illustrated by the cross of Jesus. Peacemaking (in this case between God and humanity) sometimes requires that one willingly becomes the lightening rod, absorbing the hatred that would otherwise destroy others.

sons of God. To be called a son or a child of someone meant that a person's character was seen as a reflection of the master or teacher whom he followed. It is in this sense that those who work for peace will be acknowledged to be the children of God, since God himself is the author of peace and reconciliation.

5:10 ***persecuted.*** The final beatitude focuses on the persecution that comes to those who live out the ways of God. Many first-century Christians knew what it was like to be persecuted (see 1Pe 1:6; 3:13-17; 4:12-19).

because of righteousness. This persecution comes as a result of pursuing God's way in contrast to the way of the world. The hostility Jesus encountered from the religious leaders of his time illustrates the price those who pursue God's agenda may have to pay.

kingdom of heaven. Just as this is the reward promised in the first beatitude, so it is also promised in the final beatitude. The kingdom of heaven sums up all that is involved in coming into the orbit of God and becoming part of his world.

5:11–12 This is not an additional beatitude. Rather, it is a comment on the final beatitude (v.10). The opposition in view is that which is suffered because of one's loyalty to Jesus and his kingdom. Three types of opposition are noted: insults, persecution, and lies.

5:12 ***be glad.*** This is literally "to leap exceedingly." The response of the Christian to this type of mistreatment is to be that of unrestrained joy. This is not because of a "persecution complex" that derives joy out of opposition, but out of a recognition that such mistreatment at the hands of the world is an indication that one is faithful to God.

reward in heaven. In order to avoid misusing the name of the Lord (and thus violating the third commandment—Ex 20:7), Jews commonly used the word "heaven" as a synonym for "God." Matthew follows this custom. This promise is not so much looking to a heavenly afterlife, but simply asserting that such people have a rich reward with God.

the prophets. According to Jewish tradition, Isaiah was sawn in two by those refusing to hear his prophecy; Jeremiah was stoned by his own people; Ezekiel was ridiculed; Amos was told to leave and prophesy somewhere else (Am 7:10–13). Moses,

Samuel, Elijah, and Elisha likewise met with opposition. John the Baptist was beheaded. Jesus would be crucified. The person who maintains loyalty to God needs to be reminded of the ultimate end awaiting him or her, because the possibility of opposition in this life is exceedingly high.

On Hungering and Thirsting...

The seeking of righteousness impacts our business, political, and social life every bit as much as it does our personal relationships. The call is to pursue God's agenda in *all* our dealings. "For biblical righteousness is more than a private and personal affair; it includes social righteousness as well...liberation from oppression...the promotion of civil rights, justice in the law courts, integrity in business dealings and honor in home and family affairs" (John R.W. Stott, *The Message of the Sermon on the Mount,* InterVarsity, 1978).

on seeing God . . .

"In a sense there is a vision of God even while we are in this world. Christian people can see God in nature ...the Christian sees God in the events of history ... But there is a seeing also in the sense of knowing Him, a sense of feeling He is near, and enjoying His presence.

"But of course that is a mere nothing as compared with what is yet to be ... You and I are meant for the audience chamber of God; you and I are being prepared to enter into the presence of the King of kings" (D. Martin Lloyd-Jones, *Studies in the Sermon on the Mount,* Vol. 2, Eerdmans, 1960. p. 114).

on being persecuted for righteousness . . .

"Blessed are those who die for reasons that are real, for they themselves are real.

Blessed are all those who yet can sing when all the theater is empty and the orchestra is gone.

Blessed is the man who stands before the cruelest king and only fears his God" (Calvin Miller, *The Singer,* InterVarsity, 1975, p. 70).

UNIT 3—Salt and Light/Fulfillment of the Law / Matt. 5:13–20

Scripture

Salt and Light

13 "You are the salt of the earth. But if the
salt loses its saltiness, how can it be made
salty again? It is no longer good for any-
thing, except to be thrown out and tram-
pled by men.
14 "You are the light of the world. A city on
a hill cannot be hidden. 15 Neither do people
light a lamp and put it under a bowl.
Instead they put it on its stand, and it
gives light to everyone in the house. 16 In
the same way, let your light shine before
men, that they may see your good deeds
and praise your Father in heaven.

The Fulfillment of the Law

17 "Do not think that I have come to abol-
ish the Law or the Prophets; I have not
come to abolish them but to fulfill them.
18 I tell you the truth, until heaven and earth
disappear, not the smallest letter, not the
least stroke of a pen, will by any means
disappear from the Law until everything is
accomplished. 19 Anyone who breaks one
of the least of these commandments and
teaches others to do the same will be
called least in the kingdom of heaven, but
whoever practices and teaches these com-
mands will be called great in the kingdom
of heaven. 20 For I tell you that unless your
righteousness surpasses that of the
Pharisees and the teachers of the law, you
will certainly not enter the kingdom of
heaven.

Group Questions

Every group meeting has three parts: **(1) To Begin** (15 minutes) to break the ice; **(2) Read Scripture and Discuss** (30 Minutes); and **(3) To Close and Pray** (15-30 Minutes). Try to keep on schedule. The most important time is the prayer time.

TO BEGIN / 15 Minutes (Choose 1 or 2)

- ❑ When you were growing up, how big was your family on putting up outdoor Christmas lights?
- ❑ How heavily do you use table salt? Have you ever eaten salt-free food? What did you think?!
- ❑ Are you comfortable in the "lime-light"? Or are you more at ease "back-stage"?

READ SCRIPTURE AND DISCUSS / 30 Minutes

- ❑ Salt was used in the ancient world to season, preserve and purify food. How is that symbolic of what it means to be a Christian (v. 13)?
- ❑ What does Jesus call for by telling his followers, "You are the light of the world" (v. 14)?
- ❑ How does salt become useless (see note on v. 13)? How is the purpose of light defeated (vv. 14–15)? What are the results of the absence of salt and light?
- ❑ From the allegory of salt and light, how could you make a case for Christians: Being involved in community affairs and politics? Avoiding community affairs and politics?
- ❑ Which of these best describes your "light" to the world: Floodlight—so bright I sometimes blind people? Three-way bulb—fluctuating from off to mellow to bright? Refrigerator light—subtle, but consistent when people take a close look? Flashlight—it's been awhile, but I think I can still shine?
- ❑ What did Jesus mean by saying he came to fulfill the Law and accomplish everything in it (see notes on vv. 17–18)?
- ❑ How does one obtain the level of righteousness Jesus demanded in vv. 19–20? Obeying God's law? Living by Jesus' teachings? By grace? (See note on v. 20.) How satisfied is the Lord with *your* righteousness?

TO CLOSE AND PRAY / 15-30 Minutes

- ❑ If needed, what is it going to take to get your "batteries" recharged? How can this group help you in your spiritual life?
- ❑ As "salt and light," what can your group do for a mission or outreach project?
- ❑ How would you like the group to pray for you?

Notes

5:13–16 Matthew follows up the Beatitudes with Jesus' declaration that the children of God (whom he has just described) ought to bring these qualities to the world around them. While the final beatitude described the reaction of the world to the members of the kingdom of God, these verses point out the role the members of the kingdom play in the world. While persecution may be what is in store for the believer, "aloofness or isolationism" (Hendriksen) is simply not an option for the Christian community. Instead, Christians are to be like salt (which preserves and flavors) and light (which gives illumination and insight) to the very world that so often opposes them. The Christian faith is not a pious retreat from the realities of life. Rather, it is a call to press the values of the kingdom (as reflected in the Beatitudes) into all of life's affairs.

5:13 *salt.* Salt was a basic commodity in the ancient world. It was used to season, preserve, and purify food. In the days before refrigeration, meat could be preserved indefinitely if properly salted and cured. In like manner, the children of God are to flavor the world around them with God's ways and to prevent it from going rancid. Like salt, which does its work quietly and mysteriously, so Christians are to be God's agents who combat decay and evil in the world.

loses its saltiness. Pure salt does not lose its taste. However, "what was the popularly called 'salt' was in fact a white powder (perhaps from around the Dead Sea) which, while containing sodium chloride (the chemicals which make up true salt), also contained much else since ... there were no refineries. Of this dust the sodium chloride was probably the most soluble component and so the most easily washed out. The residue of white powder still looked like salt, and was doubtless still called salt, but it neither tasted nor acted like salt. It was just road dust" (Stott).

trampled. The saltless white powder was used as a surfacing material for roads. If Jesus' followers lose their distinctive character (that is, if they fail to press after the qualities reflected in the Beatitudes), they will become useless to the world. "'What a downcome,' comments A.B. Bruce, 'from being saviours of society to supplying materials for footpaths!'" (Stott).

5:14 *light.* Light is another basic element of life. The function of light is to illuminate, to drive the darkness away. It is often used throughout the Bible as a description for God, the Messiah, or the nation of Israel (1Jn 1:5; Isa 42:6; 49:6; Jn 1:9, 8:12, 9:5). Here, it is used to describe the effect on the world of those who embrace the values of the kingdom of God. Such people will illuminate the world's darkness, bringing it light and life.

of the world. Just as Israel's original purpose was to be a nation that so reflected God's nature that the Gentile nations would be drawn to its light (Isa 49:6), so the church is to be a community whose lifestyle draws others to God. The concern of Jesus, as expressed in this saying, is not simply for one nation or type of people but for the whole world.

5:14b–15 The very purpose of light is defeated if it is hidden away. It is meant to be out in the open. Just as a city situated upon a hill cannot be hid from view, no one would think of lighting a lamp only to hide it under a bowl.

the house. Houses were typically simple one-room structures. A candle or lamp lit in any part of such a house would obviously shed light throughout the whole structure. In the same way, the character of those people who embrace God's kingdom will stand out like a light that radiates its energy throughout the whole world. Jesus' disciples are not to be secret about their discipleship, but are to live openly so that others can see who and what they are.

5:16 ***let your light shine before men.*** What constitutes the "light" of Christians is what they say and do.

praise your Father. While the eighth beatitude pointed out that persecution is one response the world will have toward those who embody the qualities of God's kingdom, here the point is made that another response will be that some people will recognize in these qualities the character of God. Such people will be led to give praise to God and come to faith in him.

5:17–20 The Christian's relationship to the OT Law was a troubling point for the early Christian communities, which were composed primarily of Jewish converts. Here, Matthew presents in general terms Jesus' relationship to the Law.

5:17 ***do not think that I have come to abolish the Law.*** The charter of the kingdom, expressed in terms of its character (vv.3-12) and mission (vv.13-16), does not do away with the Law but brings it to life. Jesus will complete the OT; he is the one to whom the OT pointed; through his ministry its intent will be fulfilled.

the Law or the Prophets. "The Law" was the way the Jews referred to the first five books of the OT (the Pentateuch), while "the Prophets" refer to the major and minor prophets as well as the historical books like Kings and Chronicles.

fulfill. By his teaching, Jesus seeks to give full expression to the intention of the Law. In contrast, for all their concern about the Law (and by their preoccupation with its details), the Pharisees and other religious leaders often overlooked its purpose. This is clearly brought out in the various examples Jesus gives in 5:21–6:18.

5:18 ***I tell you the truth.*** Literally, this is "for truly I say to you," a phrase characteristic of Jesus. No other teacher of his era was known to say this.

the smallest letter/ least stroke of a pen. Some Hebrew and Aramaic characters are distinguishable only by a small line or dot. Jesus is accenting the validity of the Law as the ethical norm of members of God's kingdom.

until everything is accomplished. This probably refers back to the phrase "until heaven and earth disappear." Until God's plan for history is complete, the ethical demands of God's law remain in force. Jesus' mission was not to alter these demands, but to call people to embrace them in a deep, internal way that would penetrate their whole being.

5:19 Jesus accents the point. The commands of the Law are eternally valid as an expression of God's nature. Anyone who minimizes them betrays his or her own lack of understanding about the nature of the kingdom.

5:20 ***the Pharisees and the teachers of the law.*** To stress the point even further, the lifestyle of the members of God's kingdom is contrasted to that of the people who were considered to be the most religious in Israel. This statement by Jesus must have shocked the disciples. If the standards of the scribes and Pharisees were not high enough to enter the kingdom, what possible hope could they have of meeting even more demanding standards?

As the following six antitheses (5:21–48) show, Jesus' conception of righteousness is not a matter of conforming to even more rules, but of stripping away external regulations altogether to focus on what is going on in one's heart.

Salt and Light

by John R.W. Stott

"The salt and light metaphors which Jesus used have much to teach us about our Christian responsibilities in the world.

a. *There is a fundamental difference between . . the church and the world.* We serve neither God, nor ourselves, nor the world by attempting to obliterate or even minimize this difference ... Probably the greatest tragedy of the church throughout its ... history has been its constant tendency to conform to the prevailing culture instead of developing a Christian counter-culture.

b. *We must accept the responsibility which this distinction puts upon us ...* The function of salt is largely negative: it prevents decay. The function of light is positive: it illumines the darkness.

"... God intends us to penetrate the world. Christian salt has no business to remain snugly in elegant little ecclesiastical salt cellars; our place is to be rubbed into the secular community, as salt is rubbed into meat, to stop it going bad...

"... Christian people should be more outspoken in condemning evil ... and alongside this condemnation of what is false and evil, we should take our stand boldly for what is true, good, and decent ... To try to improve society is not worldliness but love. To wash your hands of society is not love but worldliness.

"But fallen human beings need more than barricades to stop them becoming as bad as they could be. They need regeneration, new life through the gospel. Hence our second vocation to be 'the light of the world' ... We are called both to spread the gospel and to frame our manner of life in a way that is worthy of the gospel.

"So then we should never put our two vocations to be salt and light, our Christian social and evangelistic responsibilities, over against each other as if we had to choose between them...The world needs both. It is bad and needs salt; it is dark and needs light. Our Christian vocation is to be both" (InterVarsity Press, *The Message of the Sermon on the Mount,* 1978, p. 66–67).

UNIT 4—Anger With a Brother / Matthew 5:21–26

Scripture

Murder

21 ***"You have heard that it was said to the***
people long ago, 'Do not murder,[a] and any-
one who murders will be subject to judg-
ment.' 22But I tell you that anyone who is
angry with his brother[b] will be subject to
judgment. Again, anyone who says to his
brother, 'Raca,[c]' is answerable to the
Sanhedrin. But anyone who says, 'You
fool!' will be in danger of the fire of hell.
23"Therefore, if you are offering your gift
at the altar and there remember that your
brother has something against you, 24leave
your gift there in front of the altar. First go
and be reconciled to your brother; then
come and offer your gift.
25"Settle matters quickly with your adver-
sary who is taking you to court. Do it while
you are still with him on the way, or he
may hand you over to the judge, and the
judge may hand you over to the officer,
and you may be thrown into prison. 26I tell
you the truth, you will not get out until you
have paid the last penny.[d]

a21 Exodus 20:13 *b22* Some manuscripts *brother without cause*
c22 An Aramaic term of contempt *d26* Greek *kodrantes*

Group Questions

TO BEGIN / 15 Minutes (Choose 1 or 2)

- ❑ When you were growing up, what did your brothers, sisters or other kids do that really made you mad?
- ❑ If looks could kill, about how many life sentences would you be serving for the last month's "crimes"?
- ❑ When it comes to temper, do you have a short fuse or a long fuse? How long does it take you to try to patch things up?

READ SCRIPTURE AND DISCUSS / 30 Minutes

- ❑ After shocking his listeners by saying, "Unless your righteousness surpasses that of the Pharisees and the teachers of the law, you will certainly not enter the kingdom (5:20)," Jesus begins a series of contrasts between God's standards and what people had been taught by the religious status quo. What was the simple teaching of the scribes about murder (v. 21)?
- ❑ How did Jesus expand on the prohibition of the act of murder (see note on v. 22)?
- ❑ What specific instructions does Jesus prescribe in vv. 23–24? What attitude of the heart is he calling for?
- ❑ What is the specific instruction presented in vv. 25–26? What heart attitude is Jesus calling for here?
- ❑ What would Jesus say about our quick-to-sue society? How literally should we take his comments about settling out of court?
- ❑ Was Jesus more concerned about actions or attitudes? How about you? Why?
- ❑ Seeing that Jesus uses the word *brother* four times in this passage, are these principles aimed at all relationships, or primarily at those among believers? Why is Jesus so concerned about how his followers relate to each other and reconcile conflict?
- ❑ When one Christian offends another, which one does Jesus assign the responsibility to initiate reconciliation (vv. 23–24)?
- ❑ How do you tend to handle anger and conflict? Turn inward and absorb it? Turn outward and express it? Is Christ honored?

TO CLOSE AND PRAY / 15-30 Minutes

- ❑ What relationship in your life does this unit confront? How can this group help you and pray for you?
- ❑ What do you most appreciate about this small group?
- ❑ What other requests for prayer do you have?

Notes

5:21–26 Jesus' startling statement in verse 20 sets the stage for this and the following five sections (5:27–30, 31–32, 33–37, 38–42 and 43–48), in which he illustrates the nature of the righteousness that surpasses that of the scribes and Pharisees. These sections are known as the six antitheses, so called because each begins with the formula "You have heard … " followed by "But I tell you ..." In each case Jesus forces his audience to consider the real meaning of the Law. While verses 17–20 emphasized Jesus' continuity with the Law, this formula emphasizes his discontinuity with its interpretation. Actually, the term "antithesis" is a bit misleading, since Jesus is not contradicting all of these statements. He does not say that while the law prohibited murder, now it is all right to kill anyone who bothers you, nor does he say that while adultery used to be wrong, now it is all right to indulge one's sexual fantasies without limit! Lapide suggests that they should thus be considered *supertheses* rather than antitheses, since Jesus is intensifying the meaning of the Law. In this particular section, Jesus addresses the meaning of the commandment not to murder. While the scribes had reduced the meaning of this command to simply a prohibition of the actual act, Jesus reveals that its intent is to expose the murderous desires that are found in instances of anger, insult, ridicule, and conflict. To accent its meaning, he offers three examples of murderous relationships (5:21-22) followed by two illustrations meant to encourage the active pursuit of reconciliation (5:23-26).

5:21–22 The sixth commandment says "Do not murder" (Ex 20:13), but Jesus focuses on the inner attitudes that give rise to murder (such as anger, contempt, and slander). To accent the penalty associated with such attitudes, two contrasts are offered: (1) Those who actually commit murder are subject to judgment at a local court (v. 21), while those who nurse anger are subject to the judgment of God (v. 22a); (2) Those who outwardly defame others are subject to the judgment of the Sanhedrin (v. 22b), while those who inwardly repudiate others are subject to the judgment of hell (v. 22c).

You have heard... but I tell you. This phrase has parallels in the Talmudic writings of the rabbis. It was used when rabbis wanted to emphasize an element of interpretation related to the Law which had been neglected or overlooked by contemporary thought. In this way, the unfolding implications of the Law could be related to the ever-changing social, politi-

Notes (Continued)

cal, and cultural situations of the Jewish people. In these passages, Jesus draws out the depth of meaning behind certain laws.

5:22 ***angry.*** The Greek word used here describes deep-seated, smoldering, inner anger (rather than a flash of anger).

Raca. An Aramaic term of contempt: "You good-for-nothing," (GNB). Since the word itself is simply a transliteration of the sound made in the throat of someone preparing to spit, it carries the connotation of the offensive act of spitting in another's face.

the Sanhedrin. Even though Palestine was dominated by Roman authority at this time, the Sanhedrin (a group of seventy Jewish men), was the official ruling body of the Jews. Composed of the current high priest (as well as other high priests who had been demoted from that office by Rome), members of privileged families, family heads of various traditional tribes, Pharisees, Sadducees, and scribes, this body was responsible for administering justice in matters related to Jewish law. If witnesses were present when a person acted in such a contemptible way, the person saying (or doing) such things was subject to discipline by the Sanhedrin.

You fool! This is to demean another person's basic character. In biblical usage, to call someone a fool was to accuse him or her of being morally deficient. Since the Greek word for fool sounds very similar to that of the Hebrew word for rebel, it may be that the person is actually accused of being apostate from God. In either case, the point is that the person is viewed as being worthless, thus providing the speaker with some type of internal justification for his or her mistreatment of the person.

hell. Literally, this is Gehenna, a ravine outside Jerusalem where, in ancient times, children were once sacrificed to the god Molech (1Ki 11:7). Because of such activity, the Jews considered it a defiled place. Their only use for it was as a garbage dump which was continually burning. Gehenna became a symbol for extreme horror, the place of punishment and spiritual death. The person who allows anger to smolder within is in danger of being consumed by smoldering fires.

5:23–26 Instead of cultivating the attitudes that might lead to the actual committing of murder, members of God's kingdom are to place the highest priority upon reconciliation with one another. Verses 23–24 underscore the point that this takes precedence over acts of worship, while verses 25–26 use an illustration from the legal situation of the day to make the point.

5:23 ***altar.*** The picture is of someone going to worship at the temple in Jerusalem, the only site where sacrifices could be offered. The gift the person is taking probably would have been an animal for sacrifice.

your brother. Four times the word brother is used (vv.22, 23, 24). These principles are not so much aimed at relationships in the world, but at those within the community of the church itself. It is by practicing these principles that the church shows itself to be a radically different community from the ones found in the world.

has something against you. The responsibility for initiating reconciliation lies with the one who, whether on purpose or by accident, has offended another member of the community.

5:24 Much of the OT law dealt with matters of ceremonial worship. Proper observance of the worship traditions and regulations was very important to the Jews. While Jesus did not deny the importance of worship, his stress here is that pursuing reconciliation with someone whom one has offended takes precedence even over acts related to worship. One was not to approach God while neglecting to directly address the sin committed against another person. This was not a new emphasis. Isaiah the prophet warned the people that unless they pursued justice with one another their acts of worship were abominations in God's eyes (Isa 1:10–17). However, in Jesus' day, popular spirituality had once again been reduced to ceremonial and legal observance of the traditions.

5:25–26 The second illustration of the importance of reconciliation is drawn from the legal system, in which a person is being taken to court over a dispute. Rather than aggravating the situation (by allowing it to fester until a judge has to determine one's guilt and prescribe punishment), it would be far better to acknowledge one's wrongdoing and seek to make amends so that court action is dropped. The basic principle in both illustrations is that when we become aware that we have offended someone, we should take immediate action to seek reconciliation and restore peace.

court. The Jews were offended by the Gentile custom of having debtors thrown in jail, where it was impossible for them to earn money and so pay off their debt. Yet this is the image Jesus uses to describe the situation before God of the person who refuses to seek reconciliation.

penny. The smallest Roman coin.

Interpreting the Law

by John R.W. Stott

It is popularly thought that the six antitheses in Matthew 5 are meant to show that Jesus was somehow doing away with the Old Testament, as though he was saying, "While the Old Testament law says this, I say ... " This approach misses the point of Jesus' ministry and contradicts the strong statements recorded in 5:17–20. There is not an opposition here between the Law and the Gospel, Christ and Moses, or the Old Testament and the New. Rather, as John Stott notes, the contrast is between Christ's interpretation of the law and the scribal misinterpretations.

"What ... were the scribes and Pharisees doing? ... In general, they were trying to reduce the challenge of the law, to 'relax' (v.19) the commandments of God, and so make his moral demands more manageable and less exacting...

"What the scribes and Pharisees were doing, in order to make obedience more readily attainable, was to restrict the commandments and extend the permissions of the law. They made the law's demand less demanding and the law's permissions more permissive. What Jesus did was to reverse both tendencies. He insisted instead that the full implications of God's commandments must be accepted without imposing any artificial limits, whereas the limits which God had set to his permissions must also be accepted and not arbitrarily increased.

"What Jesus did was ... to explain the true meaning of the law with all its uncomfortable implications ... And in this matter Christian disciples must follow Christ, not the Pharisees. We have no liberty to try to lower the law's standards and make it easier to obey. That is the casuistry of Pharisees, not Christians. Christian righteousness must exceed pharisaic righteousness" (InterVarsity Press, *The Message of the Sermon on the Mount,* 1978,p. 78–80).

UNIT 5—Adultery/Divorce/Oaths / Matthew 5:27–37

Scripture

Adultery

27 "You have heard that it was said, 'Do not
commit adultery.'[a] 28 But I tell you that any-
one who looks at a woman lustfully has
already committed adultery with her in his
heart. 29 If your right eye causes you to sin,
gouge it out and throw it away. It is better
for you to lose one part of your body than
for your whole body to be thrown into hell.
30 And if your right hand causes you to sin,
cut it off and throw it away. It is better for
you to lose one part of your body than for
your whole body to go into hell.

Divorce

31 "It has been said, 'Anyone who divorces
his wife must give her a certificate of
divorce.'[b] 32 But I tell you that anyone who
divorces his wife, except for marital
unfaithfulness, causes her to become an
adulteress, and anyone who marries the
divorced woman commits adultery.

Oaths

33 "Again, you have heard that it was said
to the people long ago, 'Do not break your
oath, but keep the oaths you have made to
the Lord.' 34 But I tell you, Do not swear at
all: either by heaven, for it is God's throne;
35 or by the earth, for it is his footstool; or
by Jerusalem, for it is the city of the Great
King. 36 And do not swear by your head, for
you cannot make even one hair white or
black. 37 Simply let your 'Yes' be 'Yes,' and
your 'No,' 'No'; anything beyond this
comes from the evil one.

a27 Exodus 20:14 *b31* Deut. 24:1

Group Questions

TO BEGIN / 15 Minutes (Choose 1 or 2)

- ❑ What is your first memory of interest in the opposite sex?
- ❑ Who told you about "the birds and the bees"? Did you ask for this information?
- ❑ What promise from God, or an individual, do you hold onto with all your might?

READ SCRIPTURE AND DISCUSS / 30 Minutes

- ❑ Jesus continues to contrast God's standards with those people had been taught by tradition and the Pharisees. How did Jesus deepen the meaning of the commandment not to commit adultery (vv. 27–30)?
- ❑ Why is it difficult for most Christians to talk about sex in general, and lust in particular? Because the subject is: Inappropriate? Personal and private? Scary? Embarrassing? Associated with guilt and shame?
- ❑ Is Jesus addressing all sexual urges, or only desires for an illicit relationship (see Note on vv. 27–28)? What do you think Jesus would say about pornography, or even today's mainstream culture and media?
- ❑ What is Jesus' point in using such exaggerated language in vv. 29–30 (see Notes on 29–30)? What do you do to keep your thought life sexually pure?
- ❑ How did Jesus sharpen the focus of prevailing attitudes about divorce (some rabbis allowed it for nearly any reason) in vv. 31–32?
- ❑ Why is it in Jesus' mind that a legal divorce is not necessarily a moral divorce? How has divorce touched your life, and what should be our perspective about this subject? (See "The Difficult Subject of Divorce" at the end of the Notes, but don't let this huge issue side-track the meeting)
- ❑ What is the heart of the matter regarding oaths (vv. 33–37); See note on v. 34)? Why is keeping promises so important? What letter grade would you get for keeping promises to God? To your family? To yourself?
- ❑ Does Jesus call for more, or less, than the Pharisees?

TO CLOSE AND PRAY / 15-30 Minutes

- ❑ Where is your relationship with God right now, in marriage terms: Enjoying the honeymoon? Getting down to the nitty gritty issues? On the rocks, I'm afraid? Falling in love all over again?
- ❑ How can this group support you in prayer right now?

Notes

5:27–30 Having shown the depth of meaning behind the law's prohibition against murder (the sixth commandment), Jesus now does the same with the seventh commandment (Ex 20:14).

5:27–28 ***Do not commit adultery.*** While adultery is defined as having sexual relationships with another person's spouse, the OT law also prohibited fornication, incest, bestiality, homosexuality, and rape. The prohibition against adultery in the Ten Commandments sums up the various prohibitions against illegitimate sexual acts.

lustfully. Just as anger is at the root of murder (5:21–22), so lust is at the root of adultery. "Jesus' intention is to prohibit not a natural sexual attraction, but the deliberate harboring of desire for an illicit relationship" (France).

a woman. Probably a married woman is intended, since this is how the Greek word is generally used.

5:29-30 In these statements Jesus is, of course, speaking in hyperbole, deliberately overstating or dramatizing in order to make a point. However, in the early part of the third century, Origen, a prominent theologian, took this literally and made himself a eunuch. Such actions were prohibited by the Council of Nicea in 325 A.D. The Council understood that Jesus was speaking figuratively to accent his point that radical action must be taken to root out sin in our lives.

eye. The idea here is that if lust is stimulated via sight, then deal with lust by refusing to look at the person for whom one lusts. Jesus' point here is *not* that the problem is with the other person, but with the person who lusts.

hand. Likewise if temptation comes via touch, stop touching those whom you inwardly desire. The commands regarding the eye and the hand are part of the doctrine of mortification, or the "putting to death" that which leads to sin. It is a conscious, vigilant choice to turn away from sin and those things that draw one toward sin in order to pursue God's kingdom.

5:31–32 The third antithesis (though the formula is not exactly the same as the others) has to do with divorce. This subject follows naturally from the discussion of adultery and lust.

Notes (Continued)

5:31 In first-century Judaism divorce was allowed on the basis of Deuteronomy 24:1–4, part of which is quoted here. In Deuteronomy the issue is whether a man can remarry his wife whom he divorced (Dt 24:1–4 prohibits such remarriage). The thing to note is that in Deuteronomy, the right to divorce and the right of the wife to remarry is assumed. However, nowhere in the OT are the grounds for divorce stated. This was the subject of the debate in the first century: on what grounds could a husband divorce his wife (only husbands had the right of divorce, though in certain instances a wife could require her husband to divorce her). The stricter rabbis allowed divorce only on the basis of adultery. The more liberal teachers allowed divorce for a host of trivial reasons: e.g., if a woman spoiled her husband's dinner, or if her husband found her less attractive than someone else. To Jesus, such debate missed the point. It focused on ways a man could justify divorcing his wife, whereas Jesus' concern was with the true intention of marriage.

a certificate of divorce . In large part, the intent of the Mosiac law (see Dt 24:1-4) was to protect a woman from capricious treatment by her husband. Thus he was required to give her a certificate of divorce, thereby verifying her release from the marriage and giving her the right to remarry without the threat of being accused of adultery.

5:32 In this verse, as he has done twice already (and will continue to do as the Sermon on the Mount unfolds), Jesus goes well beyond what the Law required: anger is a form of murder (5:21–26); lust is a form of adultery (5:27–30); and here, remarriage is a form of adultery.

In each instance (murder, adultery, divorce), the question must be asked: who can live up to such high standards? (The disciples realize this in Mt 19:10, where Jesus repeats his words about divorce, and respond with amazement, "If this is the situation between a husband and wife, it is better not to marry.") But this is the point. What Jesus outlines in the Sermon on the Mount is the ideal, the goal, the standards of the kingdom. He describes what *ought* to be. There ought to be no remarriage after divorce. In fact, there ought to be no divorce (Mt 19:3–8). But, in fact, there is divorce, just as there is anger and lust. We are called to be perfect (Mt 5:48), but none of us is. Thus, we all need to ask for forgiveness on a daily basis (Mt 6:12). It is important to interpret Jesus' words about divorce and remarriage in the light of the whole Sermon on the Mount. He defines the perfect standard which we must strive to keep, and yet our fallenness keeps getting in the way of achieving such a goal.

except for marital unfaithfulness. The word which is translated "marital unfaithfulness" refers to a variety of sexual behaviors: "every kind of unlawful intercourse" according to the Greek dictionary. The question is, what is intended here? The word could refer to incestuous marriages involving blood relatives. Such arrangements were allowed by Roman law and were common in the Hellenistic world of the first century. They were, however, forbidden by OT law. Or the word could refer to adulterous relationships. The point is that divorcing an unchaste woman would not *make* her an adulteress, since she is already such, so the husband would not, in this case, be responsible for forcing her into an adulterous union (a second marriage). What is offered here is not an exception that makes divorce acceptable, only an exception to the rule that all divorce is adulterous.

causes her to become an adulteress. In traditional Judaism, a man was never guilty of adultery. He could marry other women, divorced or not (polygamy was still possible though little practiced in the first century) and he could have concubines. But a wife who had sexual relations with any other man was guilty of adultery against her husband (Guelich). But here Jesus makes the man responsible for his ex-wife's adultery (should she remarry) because he divorced her. Thus Jesus' statement is stricter than custom of the time and stricter than Dt. 24:1–4 (which clearly allows for remarriage on the part of women). Once again, as in verses 22 and 28, Jesus radicalizes OT law.

5:33–37 The fourth antithesis deals with the matter of keeping one's word.

5:33 *Do not break your oath.* Jesus does not so much quote the OT as summarize various passages on the subject of oaths (see Ex 20:7; Lev 19:12; Nu 30:2; Dt 23:21–23).

5:34 *Do not swear at all.* Jesus goes beyond the OT by pointing out the problem behind the fact that a person resorts to oath-taking in order to be trusted. He identifies a series of objects that people used to swear upon. Contrary to what the rabbis taught, according to Jesus it does not matter whether you swear upon

God's name (which was considered binding) or on anything else (a non-binding oath), since all objects are God's. His point is that a person's word alone should be sufficient to guarantee the accuracy of a statement. The issue in this passage is not so much against oath-taking (Jesus did not refuse the chief priest's command to swear an oath in 26:62–64) as it is having a character that is so full of integrity that others can trust our word without having to resort to an oath.

The Difficult Subject of Divorce

Jesus' statement on divorce in 5:31–32 needs to be understood in the context of the whole sermon. Ideally, there should be no divorce. As seen from Matthew 19 and Mark 10, divorce and remarriage is a departure from God's intention for marriage. Its presence, like the presence of anger, greed, and pride, betrays a lack of inner righteousness. Jesus' words about divorce in this context are meant to reveal yet another area where the so-called "righteousness" of the Pharisees was only skin-deep. The presence of divorce and remarriage amongst them, like lust (5:28), was indicative of the fact that in their hearts they had failed to live by the spirit of the command "Thou shall not commit adultery."

It is important to note here that while the woman is called the adulteress, the *fault* for that situation is placed upon the husband who divorced her. In that culture, a divorced woman would have little choice for survival except to marry again. Jesus is not condemning her because of that social reality, but he is pointing out to the men involved that their casual attitude towards marriage and divorce is not much more than a "legal" way of indulging in the immorality of adultery.

To the Jews of Jesus' day, divorce and remarriage were perfectly acceptable. Neither was considered a sin. For men at least, divorce and remarriage carried no moral stigma. Jesus' statement suddenly placed their attitude towards divorce and remarriage into the category of moral evil, a reality they had never before considered. While they held that their divorces and remarriages were *legal*, Jesus asserted that they were not *moral*. Their actions betrayed inner attitudes that fell far short of the quality of love for which God looks in truly "righteous" people.

Jesus' intent in the entire sermon is to demonstrate people's desperate need for grace. He is not running a campaign in which he is cataloging areas where new laws are needed, but is instead showing his disciples common examples from life which betrayed their lack of true, inner righteousness. His listeners then, as his readers now, were all touched in some way by anger, hate, an unforgiving spirit, lust, divorce, lack of integrity, lack of generosity, and so forth. His point is that these common realities are symptoms of our brokenness and need for grace. They are symptoms that we do not have it in ourselves to be righteous enough for God, no matter how clever we may be in devising justifications for these attitudes and actions.

UNIT 6—An Eye for an Eye/Love for Enemies / Matt.5:38–48

Scripture

An Eye for an Eye

38 "You have heard that it was said, 'Eye
for eye, and tooth for tooth.'[a] 39 But I tell
you, Do not resist an evil person. If someone strikes you on the right cheek, turn to
him the other also. 40 And if someone wants
to sue you and take your tunic, let him
have your cloak as well. 41 If someone
forces you to go one mile, go with him two
miles. 42 Give to the one who asks you, and
do not turn away from the one who wants
to borrow from you.

Love for Enemies

43 "You have heard that it was said, 'Love
your neighbor[b] and hate your enemy.' 44 But
I tell you, Love your enemies[c] and pray for
those who persecute you, 45 that you may
be sons of your Father in heaven. He causes his sun to rise on the evil and the good,
and sends rain on the righteous and the
unrighteous. 46 If you love those who love
you, what reward will you get? Are not
even the tax collectors doing that? 47 And if
you greet only your brothers, what are you
doing more than others? Do not even
pagans do that? 48 Be perfect, therefore, as
your heavenly Father is perfect.

a38 Exodus 21:24; Lev. 24:20; Deut. 19:21
b43 Lev. 19:18 *c44* Some late manuscripts *enemies, bless those who curse you, do good to those who hate you*

Group Questions

TO BEGIN / 15 Minutes (Choose 1 or 2)

❑ As a kid, who was your "Public Enemy #1"? Why?
❑ Did you grow up dealing with conflict more with your hands or your tongue?
❑ How did your parents settle disputes between children? How, as a parent, have you?

READ SCRIPTURE AND DISCUSS / 30 Minutes

❑ The contrasts Jesus makes between prevailing religious values and God's standards for righteousness moves to another arena. What new way of love did Jesus introduce in vv. 38–42 (see notes on vv. 38–39)?
❑ Do you think these admonitions are to be taken literally, or are they an exaggerated way of making a point (like cutting off your hand if it offends you)? If you think they're exaggerations, what does Jesus *really* mean? If you take them literally, what could be the outcome—for instance if you obeyed v. 42 without question?
❑ In v. 43 only "Love your neighbor" was from the Old Testament. "Hate your enemy" isn't found in Scripture, but was a common teaching of the day. How did Jesus correct that misunderstanding (vv. 43–48)? Who are we exempt from loving?
❑ What does this passage communicate that love involves: Humility? Prayer? Action? Unconditional positive regard? God's perfect grace?
❑ Are these teachings meant to be the basis for decisions like participating in wars and lawsuits? Why or why not?
❑ Where do you need to "turn the other cheek" on some minor issues, so that you can devote your energy to the major ones?
❑ What does Jesus mean when he tells his followers to "Be perfect" (see note on v. 48)? How is that different from "perfectionism"?

TO CLOSE AND PRAY - 15–30 Minutes

❑ How is your small group doing on the goals you set at the beginning of this course?
❑ How would you rate your week with a number between 1 and 10—1 being TERRIBLE and 10 being GREAT?
❑ How can this group pray for you today and this week?

Notes

5:38–42 The fifth antithesis has to do with revenge.

5:38 ***"Eye for eye".*** This is said to be the oldest law in the world. It is found in the codes of Hammurabi, a king who lived in the eighteenth-century B.C., as well as three times in the OT (Ex 21:23-24; Lev 24:20; Dt 19:21). The law's original context was in terms of judicial punishments. Its point was usually not to *require* "eye for eye, and tooth for tooth" but to limit punishment to the extent of the crime. Without this law, the tendency among tribal people would be for an aggrieved person to seek revenge upon his or her attacker by killing that person and, perhaps, his or her entire family! Even during the time of the establishment of the Jews as a nation, this law was not literally applied. Typically, instead of strict physical punishments, monetary reimbursements were made for offenses. Thus, by Jesus' day, no Jewish court of law literally applied this principle. However, the scribes had interpreted this judicial principle into a justification for acts of personal revenge, even though such acts were explicitly prohibited by the law (Lev 19:18)! The scribes had transformed this law that set limits on judicial actions into an individual right to carry out revenge in one's private affairs. Thus, it appeared that one could seek to do harm to another person and still be a good follower of God's law!

5:39 ***Do not resist an evil person.*** Jesus dismisses this misinterpretation of the scribes and calls instead for an attitude of non-retaliation. In this context, "to resist" means to oppose or fight back, or to seek revenge against someone who has harmed. Love, as illustrated by Jesus' response to the abuse of the Roman guards (Mt 27:27–31), absorbs and diffuses hate: It does not respond in kind (Ro 12:19–21). Jesus' teaching here does not invalidate judicial practices that seek justice for crimes. The point is that injustice and evil are to be dealt with through the proper channels, and not made into personal vendettas. Nor does Jesus' teaching imply that one should never take measures to protect oneself or someone else who is being assaulted. What is prohibited is the seeking of revenge, the desire and action to harm another in order to get back at them for a wrong done against you. What is exposed is the pharisaic hypocrisy of using the law to justify attitudes and actions the law actually prohibited.

strikes you on the right cheek. This is the first of three examples of the principle of non-retaliation in action. "The Greek verb *rhapizo* refers to striking another on the face with the back of the hand, an action which was regarded as a very great insult meriting punishment" (Hill). What seems to be in view here is actually more of a form of insult rather than an act of physical violence. It is the sort of thing a Roman soldier might do to a Jewish subject (or a master to a slave) to indicate his superior position.

the other one. Instead of retaliating or seeking action at the law court, this saying amounts to allowing the person to insult you again. The point is not that the believers are too weak or timid to fight back, but that they are so disciplined by love that they simply refuse to act in a way that fails to express love.

5:40 The second illustration comes from the law court. Rather than fighting your opponent in court, give what is sought; in fact, give even more than what is asked! The root idea here is not so much the avoidance of litigation as it is the encouragement to act with a generous, loving attitude toward all people.

tunic. This was the close fitting under-robe made of cotton or linen.

cloak. The law (Ex 22:25–26; Dt 24:10–13) prohibited a person from seizing a person's cloak as the payment of a debt, since this woolen outer robe was used as a blanket at night. Jesus' call here is for his followers to give beyond what even the law could require: They should give beyond that which is demanded.

5:41 ***forces you to go one mile.*** Roman soldiers had the right to press civilians into service to carry their gear for a distance up to one mile. The word used here is a technical term for such compulsory conscription.

mile. The Roman "mile" was 1,000 paces.

5:42 This example is drawn from the practice of lending and borrowing. The follower of Jesus is to lend to those in need regardless of their perceived ability to repay. However, as in other verses in this section, a literal application of these words in every situation is probably not in view (see vv.29–30), otherwise all those in the church would soon be reduced to total poverty and would themselves be in need of constant assistance. The aim here is to encourage a free spirit of generosity (as opposed to a narrow assessment of personal gain).

5:43–48 The sixth and final antithesis has to do with the extent of love.

5:43 ***"Love your neighbor".*** Jesus quotes Leviticus 19:18, which was the basis for community relationships among the Israelites ("Do not seek revenge or bear a grudge against one of your people, but love your neighbor as yourself").

"hate your enemy". This command is found neither in the OT nor in the Talmud. Some OT passages even call for compassion toward enemies (see Pr 25:21). However, passages that spoke of God's ultimate judicial action upon those nations which threatened Israel (see Dt 7:1–2; 20:16–18; 23:5–6; Ps 139:21) may have been misapplied in popular thought to justify personal animosity against those one disliked, especially non-Jews.

5:44 ***Love your enemies.*** Jesus expands Leviticus 19:18 to include all people in the call to love others. By this statement, he makes it clear that there is no one who stands outside the circle of love. He, in essence, redefines the whole concept of who one's neighbor is (see Lk 10:25–37).

love. The word used here is *agape*. This is love that shows itself not by what a person feels, but by what that person does. *Agape* love is benevolent action done on the behalf of another without the expectation of reward.

pray. One way this sort of love is demonstrated is by prayer for those who harass you.

5:45 Such an attitude shows one to be a child of God, because God treats all people with care, whether they are friend or enemy.

5:46 ***tax collectors.*** Tax collectors grew rich by charging people more than what was required (only *they* knew what was demanded by Rome), keeping the excess for themselves. A tax collector was, therefore, considered to be a traitor to Israel, one who was made unclean by his contact with Gentiles.

5:48 ***Be perfect.*** The Greek word used for "perfect" is *teleios*, which means "having attained the end or purpose." "A thing is perfect if it fully realizes the

TIME FOR A CHECK-UP

SEVEN COMMON SMALL GROUP AILMENTS AND HOW TO OVERCOME THEM

LET'S MAKE A SMALL GROUP
GROUP #1
GROUP #2
GROUP #3

ARE YOU FEELING A LITTLE

NERVOUS ABOUT BEING IN A SMALL GROUP?

SYMPTOMS: Do you break out into a sweat at the mention of small groups. Does your mouth turn to sawdust when it comes "your turn" to share? To pray?

PRESCRIPTION: Take this test to see if you are ready to belong to a small group. If you answer "yes" on seven out of ten questions below, you are probably ready to take the plunge.

1. Are you looking for a place where you can deal with the serious questions in your life right now? ☐ Yes ☐ No

2. Are you open to the possibility that God has something special for your life? ☐ Yes ☐ No

3. Are you open to the Bible as the source where God's will for your life can be explored? ☐ Yes ☐ No

4. Are you able to admit that you do not have all the answers about the Bible? God? Your own life? ☐ Yes ☐ No

5. Are you able to let others have questions about the Bible or God? ☐ Yes ☐ No

6. Are you willing to accept people in the group that are "Prodigal Sons" and have a long way to go in their spiritual faith? ☐ Yes ☐ No

7. Are you willing to keep anything that is shared in this group in strict confidence? ☐ Yes ☐ No

8. Are you willing to share in the responsibility for the group and to support group members with your prayers? ☐ Yes ☐ No

9. Are you willing to give priority to this group for a short period of time (such as six to twelve weeks) and consider making a longer commitment after this time? ☐ Yes ☐ No

10. Are you excited about the possibilities of belonging to a group that could make a difference in your life? ☐ Yes ☐ No

NEW YORK
PARIS
ALBUQUERQUE
TOPEKA
?
MAP

ARE YOU FEELING A LITTLE

CONFUSED ABOUT YOUR PURPOSE?

SYMPTOMS: Do you feel like you are playing on a team that doesn't have any rules? Any direction? Any idea of what you want to do or accomplish? Or where you are going?

PRESCRIPTION: Before you ever started the group, you should have decided on a COVENANT that spelled out your purpose, rules, expectations, etc. If you didn't, call "time out" and decide *together* on a covenant.

Here's how. Take the first sentence below and ask everyone to finish the sentence. Then, try to come up with a one sentence statement that you all can agree to. "The purpose of our group is . . ."

Then, take the second sentence and decide on your specific goals, etc. . . . until you have decided on your GROUP COVENANT. This becomes your game plan.

1. The purpose of our group is . . .

2. Our specific goals are . . .

3. We will meet ____________________ times, every ____________________ week, after which we will evaluate our group.

4. We will meet: Day of week ____________________ from ________ (time) to ________.

5. We will meet at ____________________, or rotate the place where we meet.

6. In addition to the study of the Bible, we will . . .

7. We will adhere to the following ground rules:
- ☐ The leader of the group will be . . . or we will rotate the leadership.
- ☐ The host for each meeting (other than the leader) will be . . . or we will rotate this responsibility.
- ☐ Food/refreshments will be . . .
- ☐ Baby-sitting, etc.

8. In addition to these general rules, we will agree to the following disciplines:
- ☐ Attendance: To give priority to the group meetings
- ☐ Participation: To share responsibility for the group
- ☐ Confidentiality: To keep anything that is said strictly confidential
- ☐ Accountability: To give permission to group members to hold you accountable for goals you set for yourself
- ☐ Accessibility: To give one another the right to call upon you for help in time of need—even in the middle of the night.

ARE YOU FEELING A LITTLE

DISTANT FROM THE OTHERS IN YOUR GROUP?

SYMPTOMS: Does your group start off like a Model A Ford on a cold morning? Or sag in the middle when you get to the Bible study? Do you find some of the people do all the talking . . . and others never get out of their "shell"?

PRESCRIPTION: Use the "flow questions" in the margin, next to the Scripture text, to guide the discussion. The questions are carefully designed to explode like time bombs on three levels of sharing: (1) TO BEGIN—to break the ice, (2) READ SCRIPTURE AND DISCUSS—to discuss the Scripture text, and (3) TO CLOSE AND PRAY—to take inventory of your own life.

1 **TO BEGIN / 10–15 Minutes:** Start off with a few good "stories" about your childhood or human-interest experiences. The better the "stories" at this level . . . the deeper the group will share at the close. (There is a close parallel between "childlikeness" and "Christlikeness".)

TO BEGIN / 15 Minutes (Choose 1 or 2)

- ❑ What mail will you open first: Bills? Official looking stuff? Personal mail? Love letter?
- ❑ When you care for someone, are you more likely to send a funny card or a touching one?

2 **READ SCRIPTURE AND DISCUSS / 30–45 Minutes:** You read the Scripture text at this point and go around on the first question. The questions are designed both to get you into the text and to help you reflect on the Scripture's meaning for your own life. The questions will help to draw your group together in a way that all can participate and share. By the way, you do not have to finish all the questions. Save time for the TO CLOSE AND PRAY section.

READ SCRIPTURE AND DISCUSS / 30 Minutes

- ❑ Where is Paul writing from? Why? Who is he writing to? (Hint: Go back and read the Introduction, especially the paragraph on Origin and Occasion.)
- ❑ Who was the Apostle Paul in your spiritual life—who introduced you to Jesus Christ and cared about your spiritual growth?

3 **TO CLOSE AND PRAY / 15–30 Minutes** This is the heart of the Bible study. The purpose is to take inventory of your own life and share with the group "what God is telling you to do." The questions are "high risk"; that is, the group is asked to share on a "need level," before moving on to prayer.

TO CLOSE AND PRAY / 15-30 Minutes

- ❑ If you had a spiritual check-up today, what would the doctor prescribe?
- ❑ How can this Bible study group help you reach your spiritual goals?
- ❑ Who is someone you would like to invite to this group next week?
- ❑ What would you like this group to remember in prayer for you this week?

Scripture

Thanksgiving and Prayer

***3**I thank my God every time I remember*
*you. **4**In all my prayers for all of you, I*
*always pray with joy **5**because of your*
partnership in the gospel from the first
*day until now, **6**being confident of this,*
that he who began a good work in you
will carry it on to completion until the
day of Christ Jesus.
***7**It is right for me to feel this way about*
all of you, since I have you in my heart;

Group Questions

TO BEGIN: What mail will you open first:Bills? Official looking stuff? Personal mail? Love letter?

READ SCRIPTURE AND DISCUSS: Where is Paul writing from? Why? Who is he writing to? (Hint: Go back and read the Introduction, especially the paragraph on Origin and Occasion).

TO CLOSE AND PRAY: If you had a spiritual check-up today, what would the doctor prescribe?

ARE YOU FEELING A LITTLE

INTIMIDATED BY THE BIBLE SCHOLARS IN YOUR GROUP?

SYMPTOMS: Are you afraid that your ignorance about the Bible could be embarrassing? For instance: if someone asked you who Melchizedek was, what would you say? If you said "an old linebacker for the Raiders", you would be wrong. Twice wrong.

PRESCRIPTION: Don't despair. Most of the people in your group don't know either. And that's O.K. This Bible study group is for BEGINNERS. And for BEGINNERS, there are Notes on the opposite page to help you keep up to speed with the rest of the group.

NOTES include:

- ☐ Definitions of significant words.
- ☐ Historical background: the political, social, economic context behind the words in the text.
- ☐ Geographical setting: facts about the country, terrain, lakes, crops, roads, and religious shrines.
- ☐ Cultural perspective: lifestyles, homes, customs, holidays, traditions, and social patterns.
- ☐ Archeological evidence: recent findings that sheds light on the Bible events.
- ☐ Summary/Commentary: recap of the argument to keep the passage in the context of the whole book.

Notes

1:3 *every time I remember you*. This is a difficult phrase to translate from the Greek. What it seems to mean is that during his times of prayer, Paul "was compelled by love to mention his Philippian friends. This means, then, that Paul gave thanks not whenever he happened to remember them, but that he regularly gave thanks for them and mentioned them to God at set times of prayer" (Hawthorne).

1:4 *with joy*. "Joy" is a theme that pervades Philippians. This is the first of some fourteen times that Paul will use the word in this epistle. He mentions "joy" more often in this short epistle

confirming the gospel. These are legal terms. The reference is to Paul's defense before the Roman court, in which he hopes to be able not only to vindicate himself and the gospel from false charges, but to proclaim the gospel in life-changing power to those in the courtroom. (See Ac 26 for an example of how Paul did this when he stood in court before Agrippa and Festus.)

1:8 *I long*. Yet another word characteristic of Paul. He uses it seven of the nine times it is found in the New Testament. This is a strong word and expresses the depth of Paul's feelings for them, his desire to be with them, and the wish to minister

KEEP OUT
SMALL GROUP IN SESSION

ARE YOU FEELING A LITTLE

TEMPTED TO KEEP THE GROUP JUST FOR YOURSELF?

SYMPTOMS: Two feelings surface: (1) if we let anyone into our group, it would destroy our "closeness", and/or (2) if we let anyone into our group, we would not have time enough to share.

PRESCRIPTION: Study the ministry of Jesus and the early church: the need for "closeness" and the danger of "closedness." How did Jesus respond to his own disciples when they asked to "stay together" and build a "monument." Note the Story of the Transfiguration in Mark 9:2-13.

SOLUTION #1: Pull up an empty chair during the prayer time at the close of the group and pray that God will "fill the chair" with someone by the next week.

SOLUTION #2: When the group reaches seven or eight in number, divide into two groups of 4—4 at the dining table, 4 at the kitchen table—when the time comes for the Bible study . . . and reshuffle the foursomes every week so that you keep the whole group intact, but sub-group for the discussion time.

THREE PART AGENDA FOR GROUP USING THE SUB-GROUP MODEL

GATHERING/15 Minutes/All Together.
Refreshments are served as the group gathers and assignments are made to sub-groups of 4.

SHARING/30-45 Minutes/Groups of 4.
Sub-groups are formed to discuss the questions in the margin of the text.

CARING/15-30 Minutes/All Together.
Regather the whole group to share prayer requests and pray.

WHY ARE THESE PEOPLE SO BORING?

ARE YOU FEELING A LITTLE

BORED WITH YOUR BIBLE STUDY GROUP?

SYMPTOMS: You feel "tired" before the meeting starts. And worse after it is over. The sharing is mostly a "head-trip". One person is absent three weeks in a row. Another is chronically late. You feel like your time could be better spent doing something else, but you don't know how to say it.

PRESCRIPTION: You may be having a group "mid-life" crisis. Here are three suggestions.

1. Call "time out" for a session and evaluate your Covenant (page 5). Are you focused on your "purpose"? Your goals? Are you sticking to your rules? Should you throw out some of your rules? (Nobody said you can't.)

2. Check to see if your group is hitting on all three cylinders for a healthy small group. (1) Nurture/Bible Study, (2) Support for one another, and (3) Mission/Task. Here's a way to test yourself.

On a scale from 1 to 10, circle a number to indicate how you feel your group is doing on each of these three cylinders.

ON NURTURE/BIBLE STUDY: Getting to know the Bible. Letting God speak to you about His plans for your life through the Scripture.

We're doing a LOUSY JOB	1	2	3	4	5	6	7	8	9	10	We're doing a GREAT JOB

ON SUPPORT: Getting to know each other. Caring about each other. Holding each other accountable for the best God has for you.

We're doing a LOUSY JOB	1	2	3	4	5	6	7	8	9	10	We're doing a GREAT JOB

ON MISSION/TASK: Reaching out to others in need. Drawing people into the group, or sponsoring another group.

We're doing a LOUSY JOB	1	2	3	4	5	6	7	8	9	10	We're doing a GREAT JOB

3. Consider the possibility that God is saying it is time to shut down the group. Take time for a party. Give everyone a chance to share what the group has meant to him/her and what he/she will remember most about the group.

ANY VOLUNTEERS...?

ARE YOU FEELING A LITTLE

ITCHY ABOUT DOING SOMETHING MORE?

SYMPTOMS: You're feeling tired of just sitting around studying the Bible. You have friends who are really hurting. Struggling. God seems to be saying something, but you don't know just what.

PRESCRIPTION: Consider the possibility that God is asking your group to split up and give birth to some new groups. Here are some steps:

1. Brainstorm together. Go around and have everyone finish the first sentence below. Then, go around on the second sentence, etc.

   I am concerned about a group for . . . (such as . . . "a group for young mothers, single parents, blended families, parents of adolescents, men at my office, young couples, empty nesters . . ." etc.).

   I wish we could . . .

   I would be willing to . . .

2. Make a list of prospects (people from the fringe of the church or outside of any church) that you would like to invite to a dinner party at which you could explain "what this Bible study group has meant to you."

3. Write each of these people a hand-written invitation on your personal stationary, inviting them to the dinner party at your home. (Don't bother to use the church bulletin. Nobody reads that.)

HOW TO TURN YOUR GROUP INTO A MISSIONARY GROUP

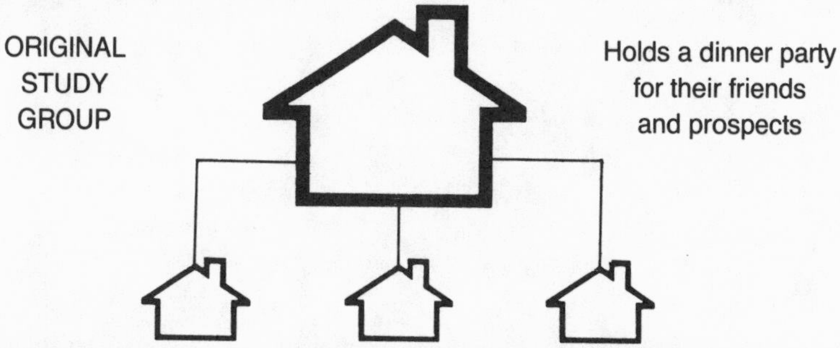

NEW STUDY GROUPS ARE FORMED/ORIGINAL GROUP THE LEADERS

(P.S. You can still get back together with the whole group once a month for a "reunion" to share exciting "stories" of your new groups.

purpose for which it was planned, and designed, and made" (Barclay). Therefore, people can be "perfect" if they realize that for which they were made. In the creation account in the OT, the purpose of men and women is stated: "God said, 'Let us make man in our image, in our likeness ... '" (Ge 1:26). Thus men and women are "perfect" when they live out God's ways and so demonstrate that they are made in his image. God's way is defined here as the way of love. This commandment to be perfect defines the goal toward which God's children strive. It is not a goal they can ever reach (only God is and can be "perfect"); it is, however, a pattern that becomes the basis of how they seek to live.

Loving One's Enemies

For people living under oppression, there may be no more disheartening words in the Bible than Jesus' command to "love your enemies." At first hearing, these words sound harsh and insensitive. Oppressed people long for release from the power of their enemies, for wrongs to be made right, and (if they will admit it) for the pleasure of seeing their oppressors humiliated as they themselves have been.

But those who have tried to live out these words of Jesus know that they are true and powerful. Perhaps no one in the 20th century has loved his enemies more courageously than Dr. Martin Luther King Jr. The famed civil rights leader understood how difficult this kind of forgiving love was. But he also saw clearly that the alternative had wide-ranging repercussions: "Returning hate for hate multiplies hate, adding deeper darkness to a night already devoid of stars..."

Hate hurts both the enemy and the victim, he said. The enemy is more than the evil deeds he does, and there is good to be found in even our worst enemy, King wrote. But hate also "scars the soul and distorts the personality" of the one who hates.[1]

When Jesus said, "I tell you, love your enemies" his first listeners knew that he was speaking from experience. Jesus knew what it was like to be despised and rejected. Everywhere he went, he faced criticism, ridicule, and devious plots to lure him into saying or doing something that could be used against him in court. The religious leaders tried to find evidence that he had broken the law. They "charged" him with blasphemy (Luke 5:21), failing to fast (Luke 5:33), collecting food on the Sabbath (Luke 6:2), and healing on the Sabbath (Luke 6:11).

Later these same listeners would see Jesus live out these words through trial, persecution, and finally death on the cross. Yet, among his final words was a prayer for his enemies: "Father, forgive them, for they do not know what they are doing" (Luke 23:34).

UNIT 7—Giving to the Needy / Matthew 6:1–4

Scripture

Giving to the Needy

6 ***"Be careful not to do your 'acts of righteousness' before men, to be seen by them.
If you do, you will have no reward from
your Father in heaven.***
***2"So when you give to the needy, do not
announce it with trumpets, as the hypocrites do in the synagogues and on the
streets, to be honored by men. I tell you
the truth, they have received their reward
in full. 3But when you give to the needy, do
not let your left hand know what your right
hand is doing, 4so that your giving may be
in secret. Then your Father, who sees what
is done in secret, will reward you.***

Group Questions

TO BEGIN / 15 Minutes (Choose 1 or 2)

- ❑ In your home, was "religion" openly expressed or more of a private matter?
- ❑ Have you ever received rewards like trophies, ribbons or plaques? Where are they now?
- ❑ How do you feel and respond when you pass a Salvation Army bell-ringer at Christmas?

READ SCRIPTURE AND DISCUSS / 30 Minutes

- ❑ The Sermon on the Mount now moves to specific areas of religious practice in which Jesus calls his disciples to an expression of righteousness surpassing that of the Pharisees (see Matt. 5:20, p. 18). As an introduction, what does Jesus say *not* to do (v. 1)?
- ❑ How do you resolve the seeming discrepancy between v. 1 and Jesus' command, "Let your light shine before men, that they may see your good deeds" (5:16)?
- ❑ According to this passage, what are the incorrect and the correct ways of giving to the needy?
- ❑ How can giving today, even to worthwhile causes, fall into "blowing your own horn"?
- ❑ What does Jesus mean when he says "do not let your left hand know what your right hand is doing" (v. 3)? Does this invalidate discussing and planning gifts, and "pledging" (see note on v. 3)? Why or why not?
- ❑ What is the reward for hypocritical giving (v. 2)? What is the reward for giving "in secret" (v. 4)? Do you *earn* this righteousness by performing secret acts of righteousness, or do you receive it as a gift *given* to you because you recognize your spiritual poverty and dependence?
- ❑ What is the challenge of this unit for *you*? To give more? Give in a different way or for different reasons? Find opportunities to give to the needy? Other?
- ❑ How are you dealing with all the strong teaching of Jesus from the Sermon on the Mount: I'm listening? I'm getting a little tired of it? I'm challenged to make changes? I'd rather pretend I don't need to change?

TO CLOSE AND PRAY / 15-30 Minutes

- ❑ What have you given and what have you received from this group? Which feels better to you?
- ❑ Do you feel like you are doing more giving or receiving in your relationship with God right now?
- ❑ How can this group care for you and pray for you?

Notes

6:1–18 Throughout 5:21–48, Jesus contrasted the righteousness of the scribes and Pharisees with that of his followers in terms of their attitudes toward general ethical practices. In this section, he shows how the surpassing righteousness (5:20) he is calling for relates to three specific examples of common Jewish piety: almsgiving (6:1–4), prayer (6:5–15), and fasting (6:16–18). In each case, Jesus first identifies the wrong way to go about such acts of devotion, and then he gives the right way.

6:1 Jesus first defines in general terms what one must not do—namely, not make a public display of religious devotion.

acts of righteousness. This is the same word found in 5:20, but the context indicates that the emphasis is on the religious activities commonly associated with moral righteousness. While there were a variety of Jewish sects which emphasized different points of faith and practice, all sects observed the three marks of righteousness spoken of in verses 1–18. The fact that Jesus' disciples did *not* practice fasting (like the Pharisees or the disciples of John the Baptist) was a point of criticism by those who could not conceive of a religious devotion that was not marked by this practice (Mk 2:18ff.).

to be seen by them. At first sight these words appear to contradict (Jesus') earlier command to 'let your light shine before men, that they may see... ' (5:16). In both verses he speaks of doing good works 'before men' and in both the objective is stated, namely in order to be 'seen' by them. But in the earlier case he commands it, while in the latter one he prohibits it. How can this discrepancy be resolved? ... The clue lies in the fact that Jesus is speaking against different sins. It is our human cowardice which made him say "Let your light shine before men', and our human vanity which made him tell us to beware of practicing our piety before men. A.B. Bruce sums it up well when he writes that we are to '*show* when tempted to hide' and '*hide* when tempted to show'. Our good works must be public so that our light shines; our religious devotions must be secret lest we boast about them" (Stott).

reward. The reward from the Father is the fullness of the kingdom (5:3). This is not something one *earns* by performing secret acts of righteousness; rather, it is a gift *given* to those who recognize their spiritual poverty. Those who perform acts of religious devotion in order to impress God and others show that they have not yet come to grips with their spiritual bankruptcy. Thus, there is no promise from God for them. In contrast, true almsgiving, prayer, and fasting is a mark of one's grateful, heart-felt response to God's graciousness and mercy. To such people the promise of the kingdom is given.

6:2–4 One of the most important first-century religious duties was giving to the poor. Jesus uses a couple of humorous images to communicate that this must not be done with the desire to be congratulated by others or even oneself. It should not be a self-centered matter, but rather an act that simply reflects one's inner loyalty to God.

6:2 *announce it with trumpets.* At certain feast times, trumpets would be blown as a way of calling people to gather for the feast. At other occasions, such as in times of famine, a trumpet would be blown so that the poor might know where to gather in order to receive food donated by a wealthy person. However, the blowing of horns before giving alms was not a regular event. Jesus uses the image metaphorically (like our phrase "he's just blowing his own horn") to accent the ostentatious display certain people made when they made their contributions. Their concern was not with glorifying God nor with caring for the needy, but with making sure that others knew they were performing their religious obligations.

the hypocrites. This is a favorite term for Matthew, who uses it 13 times (e.g., 7:5; 15:7–9; 22:18; 23:14–29). While most translations and commentaries translate this like the NIV version, Albright and Mann make a strong case that the term in Jesus' day did not connote the idea of a play-actor which we typically think of as a hypocrite. In Jesus' day, they contend, the word carried the sense of one who was overly scrupulous. In 7:5 and 15:7-9, for example, the Pharisees' preoccupation with the details of their tradition blinded them to the fact that they were in reality violating God's law. The point is that the Pharisees were not being rebuked for consciously playing a role they knew did not match their real beliefs, but for failing to see the forest (the intent of God's law) because of their preoccupation with the trees (the details of their traditions). In this incident, it was not their lack of inner conviction that Jesus is faulting (they undoubtedly sincerely believed they ought to give to the poor), but the fact they wanted to make sure that their scrupulous observance of the traditions was seen by others.

they have received their reward in full. A sense of smug self-satisfaction and temporary honor received from others they have impressed is the only reward these people will get. There is nothing eternal or spiritual about it whatsoever.

6:3 *do not let your left hand know what your right hand is doing.* This is another humorous, graphic illustration used to stress the point that giving is to be viewed as an act between the giver and God. The issue is not whether one gives in public versus in private, but the attitude with which one gives at all. The point of this teaching is not to rule out the pledge systems frequently used by churches so that they can form responsible budgets, nor to invalidate the importance of discussion in a family about its giving priorities. What is rejected here is the motivation of giving with the calculated desire to prove to others (v.2) *or* to oneself (vv.3–4) that one is righteous. While the gift still is of use to the recipient, under those types of circumstances it has no value for the person who gave. In contrast, the proper attitude for giving is seen in the story of the poor widow who, with no thought of impressing others nor any pretensions about being able to earn anything from God, gave all she could for the sake of others out of a heart of love and gratitude (Lk 21:1–4).

6:4 *in secret.* This reinforces the unselfconscious giving reflected in verse 3 about not letting the left hand know what the right hand is doing. "What is it to perform acts of love in secret? The secret place is the centered place ... to be contrasted with the merely external dimension of human existence. From beginning to end, the Sermon on the Mount attempts to draw the distinction between the center and the periphery of human existence: the central problem to be confronted is not murder, but the anger of the soul; the crucial problem is not adultery and divorce, but the attitude of the lustful heart; and since this is so, when acts of charity are performed, the most important fact about them is not their external expression, but the centered self from which they spring. Where do acts of charity originate? Jesus tells us that if they are to be authentic, they must originate from the secret place ... the centered place where God himself promises to be present" (Vaught).

Notes

On Rewards . . .

Nobody talks very much about heavenly rewards these days, at least not in Western countries. Pride keeps some people from admitting they need or desire anything more than they already have. A false understanding of humility makes others believe it's wrong even to think about being rewarded by God.

Perhaps the problem lies in a confusion about the difference between *rewards* and *earnings.* Of course, no one can *earn* God's acceptance by good works. Salvation is a "gift of God;" it is "not by works" (Eph. 2:8,9). The Christian's good works are to be an expression of thanks to God for what he has already done in Christ, not payment for a ticket into his presence. God also freely expresses his appreciation through gifts of love. Throughout Scripture, God promises that he will reward, or "bless," those who are faithful.

C.S. Lewis, in reflecting on Jesus' promise of rewards in Matthew 6:1-4, puts the matter of rewards into a proper perspective:

> "If we consider the unblushing promises of reward and the staggering nature of rewards promised in the Gospels, it would seem that Our Lords finds our desires, not too strong, but too weak. We are half-hearted creatures, fooling about with drink and sex and ambition when infinite joy is offered us, like an ignorant child who wants to go on making mud pies in a slum because he cannot imagine what is meant by the offer of a holiday at the sea. We are far too easily pleased." (C.S. Lewis, *The Weight of Glory,* Eerdmans, 1975.)

UNIT 8—Prayer/Fasting / Matthew 6:5–18

Scripture

Prayer

5 “And when you pray, do not be like the
hypocrites, for they love to pray standing
in the synagogues and on the street cor-
ners to be seen by men. I tell you the truth,
they have received their reward in full. 6 But
when you pray, go into your room, close
the door and pray to your Father, who is
unseen. Then your Father, who sees what
is done in secret, will reward you. 7 And
when you pray, do not keep on babbling
like pagans, for they think they will be
heard because of their many words. 8 Do
not be like them, for your Father knows
what you need before you ask him.
9 “This, then, is how you should pray:
“ ‘Our Father in heaven,
hallowed be your name,
10 your kingdom come,
your will be done
on earth as it is in heaven.
11 Give us today our daily bread.
12 Forgive us our debts,
as we also have forgiven our debtors.
13 And lead us not into temptation,
but deliver us from the evil one.[a]’
14 For if you forgive men when they sin
against you, your heavenly Father will also
forgive you. 15 But if you do not forgive men
their sins, your Father will not forgive your
sins.

Fasting

16 “When you fast, do not look somber as
the hypocrites do, for they disfigure their
faces to show men they are fasting. I tell
you the truth, they have received their
reward in full. 17 But when you fast, put oil
on your head and wash your face, 18 so that
it will not be obvious to men that you are
fasting, but only to your Father, who is
unseen; and your Father, who sees what is
done in secret, will reward you.

a13 Or *from evil*; some late manuscripts *one, / for yours is the kingdom and the power and the glory forever. Amen.*

Group Questions

TO BEGIN / 15 Minutes (Choose 1 or 2)

- ❑ How long could you make it without ice cream?
- ❑ What rote prayers were you taught as a child?
- ❑ Who is an example to you of a person whose daily life is molded by prayer?

READ SCRIPTURE AND DISCUSS / 30 Minutes

- ❑ Jesus now turns to the practices of prayer and fasting in his call to "surpassing righteousness." Who does he warn *not* to pray like (vv. 5–8)?
- ❑ What was wrong with prayers of the "hypocrites" (see note on vv. 5–15)? What was wrong with the prayers of the "pagans" (see note on v. 7)?
- ❑ What did Jesus say is the right way to pray (v. 6)? Does this nullify public prayer? Why (see note on v. 6)?
- ❑ If God "knows what you need before you ask him" (v. 8), why is it still important to pray (see note on v. 8)?
- ❑ What significance might the plural pronouns in the so called Lord's Prayer (vv. 9–13) carry? What three concerns, related to God, should we pray about first (vv. 9–10)? What three personal concerns are to be expressed next (vv. 11–13)?
- ❑ What is the relationship between forgiveness and prayer (vv. 12–15; see note on v. 12)?
- ❑ What is the difference between Pharisee-type fasting and the fasting Jesus calls for (vv. 16–18)? How does this fasting fit in with the rest of chapter 6 (see note on vv. 16–18)?
- ❑ What "spiritual disciplines" are valued in your circles? How can they be misused to impress others? Have you given in to that temptation? If so, why?
- ❑ What letter grade would you give your prayer life? What would it take to move up a grade: More closet time? More closet space (privacy)? More words? More discipline? More forgiving on my part? More "us" and "our" (less "me" and "my") prayers?

TO CLOSE AND PRAY / 15-30 Minutes

- ❑ If you took a full day for prayer and fasting, where would you go and how would you use the time? What is keeping you from doing it?
- ❑ If you went right now, what would be your most urgent prayer topic? How can this group agree with you in prayer?

Notes

6:5–15 Jesus now focuses attention on prayer, a second common element found in all forms of Jewish piety (see note on 6:1–18 and 6:1).

synagogues and on the streets. Pious Jews would recite certain prayers at sunrise, about 9 AM, at noon, at 3 PM (Ac 3:1), and at sunset. When the appointed hour for prayer came, they would simply stop where they were and pray. Jesus did not object to this practice in and of itself. What he was condemning was the fact that some people would make a *point* of being in a public place when it came time to pray so that others might observe how devout they were.

6:5 hypocrites. See note on 6:2 (p. 36).

they have received their reward in full. See note on 6:2 (p. 36).

6:6 *go into your room, close the door.* Jesus' point is not to do away with public prayer (which he practiced himself), but to stress that prayer is to be rooted in a desire to commune with God, not in a desire to make a public display of religiosity. Corporate, public prayer (as demonstrated throughout the history of Jewish and Christian practice) is perfectly legitimate when approached with this attitude.

in secret. See note on 6:4 (p. 36). "... the secret place was not the room, but the center of the person ... seeking communion with God" (Vaught).

6:7 *do not keep on babbling like pagans.* While the conspicuous prayer habits of the Pharisees are to be rejected, so are the meaningless, repetitive prayers of the pagans. God does not need to be awakened, impressed, or persuaded by us to act in accord with our needs. Christian prayer is not an attempt to manipulate God to do our bidding. It is not the mindless and mechanical repetition of many words in an attempt to impress or assuage a deity. Instead, it is a form of communication between a person and a loving, gracious God who is already predisposed to do good to those who call upon him.

6:8 *your Father.* The word here is *Abba,* an intimate term used by a child of his or her father. It is a common NT way of addressing and picturing God. For members of the kingdom, God is not primarily Judge (with its implication of moral censure), nor even Creator (with its sense of transcendent, impersonal power), but Father—a term meant to convey the warmth, intimacy, and care that is reflected in families where the father fulfills his role as a parent. Especially in the context of this Sermon, the image of Father is meant to convey a picture of one who lovingly provides for all our needs (5:45; 6:26, 33; 7:11).

knows... before you ask. This is not meant to indicate that prayer is unimportant, but rather to stress the intimate concern and awareness God has for his people. Prayer, like a child's communication with his or her father, serves to nurture the relationship between ourselves and God as it allows us to glimpse God's heart and mind.

6:9–15 The fact that the so-called Lord's Prayer is found in a shorter form and in another context in Luke 11:2-4 indicates that it was meant more as a guide to shape our private and corporate prayers rather than as a liturgical form to be mechanically repeated in worship services. It consists of three petitions that relate to God and his kingdom and three requests that deal with the everyday needs of life as disciples pursue the kingdom. The prayer suggests the kinds of things that ought to occupy the content of the prayers of God's people.

6:9 ***Our Father.*** The address stresses not only intimacy with God (by use of the word *Abba*), but also the corporate nature of the disciples' relationship with one another.

in heaven. This does not "locate" God somewhere beyond space, but stresses his majesty and dignity.

hallowed be your name. The first petition is that the name of God might be held in honor by all. The "name" of someone is a shorthand way of expressing that person's character and nature. The utmost concern for the disciple is that all he or she does is to be done to the glory of God, whose "name" he or she bears. This petition also reaches out from beyond that personal concern to include the desire that God be honored and worshiped by all peoples everywhere.

6:10 ***your kingdom come.*** The second petition expresses the vision that is to motivate the people of God. Their hope is rooted in the eschatological hope that God's kingdom will indeed one day be fully manifest and all people will know him to be king. To pray this petition is a revolutionary action. It expresses one's ultimate loyalty to God above all other forces that compete for the allegiance of a disciple.

your will be done. God's kingdom is in evidence wherever his will is being followed.

on earth as it is in heaven. This qualifies each of the three requests: in heaven his name is honored, his kingdom has come, and his will is done. The essence of these three requests is the heartfelt desire for this same reality to prevail here on earth.

6:11–13 The three requests reflect the disciples' dependency upon God to provide the physical, spiritual, and moral resources necessary to honor God's name, pursue his kingdom, and live in accordance with his will.

6:11 ***our daily bread.*** The first request is for "everything necessary for the preservation of this life, like food, a healthy body, good weather, house, home... good government and peace" (Luther). It reflects a day-by-day dependence upon God as the one who provides for our needs.

6:12 ***Forgive us.*** The second request is an acknowledgement that all people sin and thus are in need of God's daily forgiveness.

debts. Sin is seen as a debt (in that it represents a loss before God that we cannot repay).

as we also have forgiven. This is not in any way a "bargain" with God, as if the disciple is to wring forgiveness out of God by especially good behavior. It simply is a reflection that the recognition of our great debt before God is what moves us to freely forgive those who have sinned against us.

6:13 ***lead us not into temptation.*** The word *temptation* is better understood here as *test* or *trial.* Testings of our faith are sure to come. The request is not a plea to be exempt from the common moral struggles of life, but that God would empower the disciple to have the moral strength to resist giving in to evil during such struggles.

deliver us from the evil one. The evil one (the devil) is the real source of temptations.

6:14–15 See note on 6:12.
6:16–18 The third and final section concerning reli-

gious obligations has to do with fasting. The issue is not whether disciples should fast. The question is how one goes about fasting. Since the purpose of fasting is to focus one's attention and energy on God, Jesus teaches that his disciples should not fast in a way so as to draw attention to themselves.

fast. Fasting was an important part of Jewish religious celebration. Jews fasted on the Day of Atonement as well as at other special times (see Dt 9:9; 1Sa 31:13; Ps 35:13). The Pharisees made a practice of fasting twice a week. To fast meant to abstain from food from sunup to sundown.

disfigure. Literally, this means "to make invisible." This refers to the custom when fasting of putting ashes on the head (which would dirty and cover up one's face) or covering one's face with a cloth.

their reward in full. Once again, as with giving and with prayer (6:1, 2, 5), those who play to the crowds and are applauded by them for being "righteous" have received all the reward they will get.

put oil on your head and wash your face. Oil was a commonly used cosmetic. The followers of Jesus are to give no outward indication that they are engaged in a fast.

Differences in Prayer . . .

by John R.W. Stott

"...the fundamental difference between various kinds of prayer is in the fundamentally different images of God which lie behind them. The tragic mistake of the Pharisees and pagans, of hypocrites and heathen, is to be found in their false image of God. Indeed, neither is really thinking of God at all, for the hypocrite thinks only of himself while the heathen thinks of other things ... Is God a commodity that we can use him to boost our own status, or a computer that we can feed words to him mechanically?

"... We need to remember that (God) loves his children with most tender affection, that he sees his children even in the secret place, that he knows his children and all their needs before they ask him, and that he acts on behalf of his children by his heavenly and kingly power" (*The Message of the Sermon on the Mount,* InterVarsity, 1978, p. 152).

UNIT 9—Treasures in Heaven / Matthew 6:19–24

Scripture

Treasures in Heaven

19 *“Do not store up for yourselves trea-*
sures on earth, where moth and rust
destroy, and where thieves break in and
steal. 20 *But store up for yourselves trea-*
sures in heaven, where moth and rust do
not destroy, and where thieves do not
break in and steal. 21 *For where your trea-*
sure is, there your heart will be also.
22 *“The eye is the lamp of the body. If your*
eyes are good, your whole body will be
full of light. 23 *But if your eyes are bad, your*
whole body will be full of darkness. If then
the light within you is darkness, how great
is that darkness!
24 *“No one can serve two masters. Either*
he will hate the one and love the other, or
he will be devoted to the one and despise
the other. You cannot serve both God and
Money.

Do Not Worry

25 *“Therefore I tell you, do not worry about*
your life, what you will eat or drink; or
about your body, what you will wear. Is not
life more important than food, and the
body more important than clothes? 26 *Look*
at the birds of the air; they do not sow or
reap or store away in barns, and yet your
heavenly Father feeds them. Are you not
much more valuable than they? 27 *Who of*
you by worrying can add a single hour to
his life[a]*?*
28 *“And why do you worry about clothes?*
See how the lilies of the field grow. They
do not labor or spin. 29 *Yet I tell you that*
not even Solomon in all his splendor was
dressed like one of these. 30 *If that is how*
God clothes the grass of the field, which is
here today and tomorrow is thrown into
the fire, will he not much more clothe you,
O you of little faith? 31 *So do not worry,*
saying, ‘What shall we eat?’ or ‘What shall
we drink?’ or ‘What shall we wear?’ 32 *For*
the pagans run after all these things, and
your heavenly Father knows that you need
them. 33 *But seek first his kingdom and his*
righteousness, and all these things will be
given to you as well. 34 *Therefore do not*
worry about tomorrow, for tomorrow will
worry about itself. Each day has enough
trouble of its own.

[a]27 Or *single cubit to his height*

Group Questions

TO BEGIN / 15 Minutes (Choose 1 or 2)

❑ As a kid, where did you stash your special stuff?
❑ Have you ever worked more than one job? How are you at giving both your best effort?
❑ What measures have you taken to try to prevent your home, business or car from being broken into?

READ SCRIPTURE AND DISCUSS / 15 Minutes

❑ Jesus now focuses on how true righteousness differs from selfish materialism. In 6:1–18 the contrast was between earthly and heavenly rewards. What is contrasted in vv. 19–21?
❑ What is the difference between treasures on earth and treasures in heaven? Which is more secure?
❑ Can someone who isn't wealthy be just as guilty of storing up treasures on earth as a rich person? If so, how?
❑ What are some examples of storing up treasures in heaven (see Note on v. 20)? What are you doing in your life to store up such treasures?
❑ When you were growing up, did you buy into the American dream that defines success on the number of possessions you can accumulate?
❑ Who do you admire today for the non-material lifestyle they exhibit?
❑ Do you worry about your retirement plan ... or lack of it?
❑ In light of v. 24, how would Jesus respond if you told him you have no problem giving allegiance to both him *and* wealth (see note on v. 24)?
❑ How would Jesus function as a personal stockbroker? An investment banker? A telemarketer for charities? A car salesman?
❑ If you could have a chat with Jesus, what would you ask him regarding this unit—e.g. What should I do with my desires to provide a comfortable lifestyle for my family? Save for my children's future? Prepare for retirement, etc.?

TO CLOSE AND PRAY / 15-30 Minutes

❑ How well is this group "bonding"?
❑ Is your group willing to commit all these challenges from the Sermon on the Mount to the Lord?
❑ What other prayer requests would you like to share?

Notes

6:19–34 While 6:1–18 concentrated on how true righteousness (5:20) differs from the self-serving legalism of the Pharisees, here the emphasis is on how this righteousness differs from the self-absorbed materialism of the Gentiles (v.32). Just as the knowledge that "your Father, who sees what is done in secret" (v.18) frees us from having to make a public spectacle of religious practices, so, too, the knowledge that "your heavenly Father knows that you need them" (v.32) frees us from from having to be absorbed with how to provide for our material needs. Discipleship to Jesus means the believer must choose between two treasures (6:19–21), two visions (6:22–23), two masters (6:24), and two attitudes (6:25–34).

6:19–21 In 6:1–18 the contrast is between earthly and heavenly reward. Here the contrast is between earthly and heavenly treasure.

6:19 ***for yourself.*** Possessions as such are not forbidden, nor is the provision for family needs proscribed (see Pr 6:6ff.). What is incompatible with seeking God's kingdom is the obsessive pursuit of accumulating wealth or possessions as a means of trying to obtain security in life.

treasures on earth. These are any material treasures which, by their very nature, are subject to theft, corrosion, decay, and loss.

moth and rust. Literally, this is "moths and eating" (Mounce). Since rich, elaborate clothes were one mark of a person's wealth, the phrase is probably meant to point out how such garments can be destroyed by moths, mice or other vermin. In the days before mothballs, cedar closets, and steel safes, the irony of building one's life around one's possessions was that even the most valuable treasures on earth were vulnerable to destruction by insignificant creatures like moths and mice. Even with today's protective devices, inflation, devaluation, stock market crashes, economic shocks, etc. can despoil a person's earthly treasures literally overnight. Such treasures, by their very nature, are not permanent.

thieves. There were no security systems to prevent thieves from breaking in and stealing whatever valuables a person might try to hide in his or her house.

Notes (Continued)

6:20 ***treasures in heaven.*** Such treasures include the development of a Christlike character (since all we can take with us to heaven is ourselves); the increase of faith, hope, and charity, all of which (Paul said) 'abide' (1Co 13:13); growth in the knowledge of Christ whom one day we shall see face to face; the active endeavor (by prayer and witness) to introduce others to Christ, so that they, too, may inherit eternal life; and the use of our money for Christian causes, which is the only investment whose dividends are everlasting" (Stott). Disciples "store up" these treasures by an obedient way of life.

6:21 The real issue is not about the size and amount of one's possessions, but one's devotion to them. While a wealthy person's obsession with material goods might be more obvious, people of modest means can also have their lives revolve around trying to maintain or augment the few possessions they have. "Our treasure may ... be small and inconspicuous, but its size is immaterial; it all depends on the heart ... And if we ask how we are to know where our hearts are, the answer is ... simple—everything which hinders us from loving God above all things and acts as a barrier between ourselves and our obedience to Jesus is our treasure, and the place where our heart is" (Bonhoeffer). What people occupy themselves with reveals the intents and character of their motivations. This passage reveals that material possessions have the power to command a loyalty which rightly belongs to God. This theme will be expanded upon in the next two sayings.

6:22–23 The next comparison is between a good eye (lit. an eye that is "single") and a bad eye (literally, an "evil" eye).

The eye is the lamp of the body. As a light shows us the way through the darkness, so the eye is what allows us to see so that we might move and act freely. Both eye and heart are sometimes used in the Bible as a metaphor to describe the motivating principle that guides the way a person lives (e.g., note the parallelism in Psalm 199:36–37: "Turn my *heart* toward your statutes and not toward selfish gain. Turn my *eyes* away from worthless things ... "). To have a good eye is to have a pure heart. The image of an "evil eye" was used to describe those who were greedy or stingy, thus the "good eye" refers to people who have a generous spirit that leads them to share their material possessions. The contrast, therefore, is between those who seek the true goal which is obedience to God and those who lead "a life in the dark, like a blind man, because the 'evil eye' of selfishness gives no light to show the way" (France). "... just as blindness leads to darkness, so an ignoble and selfish ambition (e.g., to lay up treasures for ourselves on earth) plunges us into moral darkness" (Stott).

6:24 The contrast here is between competing masters. In one of his most memorable phrases, Jesus points out that it is impossible for a person to serve two masters.

serve. Literally, this is "to be a slave of." While a person might work for two employers, he or she cannot belong to two owners.

hate. This is not so much active dislike as it is a way of expressing the fact that loyalty to the one master makes loyalty to another master literally impossible.

Money. From *mamonas*, an Aramaic word that means possessions. God, who calls his people to "have no other gods besides me" (Ex 20: 3), will not tolerate divided loyalty from his people. Such divided loyalty is tantamount to idolatry (Eph 5:5).

Material World

James Paternoster says materialism is "more than just our tendency to buy more than we should. It's our tendency to buy a false world view which places material things at the center of life." He goes on to say:

"... advertising (is) one of the most powerful channels through which the seeds of materialism are sown in our lives. Advertisers work on the assumption that in a world of competing products, they must present their product as the answer to our desires, felt needs and fears.

"Admittedly some of the ads we see are fairly straightforward. Paper towels do absorb spills, and fabric softeners soften fabrics. But what about the connection between toothpaste and romance, or credit cards and the good life, or beer and meaningful friendships?

"The contrast is clear. Both paths require devotion and effort. Both are exclusive of the other. Jesus says that our needs for warmth, love, self-esteem, purpose, hope, happiness, and meaningful productivity all are met only as we seek after God and his ways above all else. Much of society is devoted to saying that such needs can be met through what we own, how much we own, and who knows what we own! As someone said, 'My whole life is spent spending money I don't have to buy things I don't want to impress people I don't like!' "

How can we combat such pervasive materialism? Paternoster offers three suggestions:

(1) Expose the false pretenses in ads. "There is nothing you can buy that will give you love, bring you happiness, ensure your success or make you the person you desire to be."

(2) Consciously oppose the materialistic lie by filling our minds with God's truth. "Here's a simple way to explore the conflict. Make a list of all the values and desires that you have noticed ads promoting. Now ... read Matthew 5–7 and Galatians 5. List those qualities described as good and those described as evil in those passages. Then compare your two lists, noting which values and desires fall into the following categories: those commended by Jesus or Paul and featured in ads; those commended by Jesus or Paul but absent from ads; those values commended in ads but absent from or condemned by Jesus or Paul."

(3) "Remember: renewing our minds is hard work. Companies with things to sell us work very hard to influence our thinking. We must work just as hard at studying God's word and spending time in conversation with him. We can help one another combat materialism by praying for each other, examining the messages we're receiving together and keeping one another accountable for our attitudes and day-to-day decisions about money ... our goal is not to shun all material objects, but to enjoy them for what they truly are."[1]

Ron Sider writes of how John Wesley practiced the commitment called for in this passage. Wesley taught:

"Christians should give away all but 'the plain necessaries of life' —that is, plain wholesome food, clean clothes and enough to carry on one's business. One should earn what one can, justly and honestly. Capital need not be given away. But all income should be given to the poor after one satisfies bare necessities.

"Wesley lived what he preached. Sales of his books often earned him 1,400 pounds annually, but he spent only 30 pounds on himself. The rest he gave away ... . 'If I leave behind me 10 pounds,' he once wrote, 'you and all mankind bear witness against me that I lived and died a thief and a robber.'

"What is the secret of such carefree living? ... We must genuinely want to seek first the kingdom of heaven ... Like the rich young ruler and Zacchaeus, we must decide between Jesus and riches ... Either Jesus and his kingdom matter so much that we are ready to sacrifice everything else, including our possessions, or we are not serious about Jesus."

[1]James Paternoster, *Materialism: Breaking Free From Madison Avenue's Grip,* Student Leadership Journal, IVCF, Fall 1990.
[2]Adapted from Ron Sider, *Rich Christians in an Age of Hunger,* 1990, Word, Inc.

UNIT 10—Do Not Worry / Matthew 6:25–34

Scripture

Do Not Worry

[25]*"Therefore I tell you, do not worry about*
your life, what you will eat or drink; or
about your body, what you will wear. Is not
life more important than food, and the
body more important than clothes? [26]*Look*
at the birds of the air; they do not sow or
reap or store away in barns, and yet your
heavenly Father feeds them. Are you not
much more valuable than they? [27]*Who of*
you by worrying can add a single hour to
his life[a]*?*
[28]*"And why do you worry about clothes?*
See how the lilies of the field grow. They
do not labor or spin. [29]*Yet I tell you that not*
even Solomon in all his splendor was
dressed like one of these. [30]*If that is how*
God clothes the grass of the field, which is
here today and tomorrow is thrown into
the fire, will he not much more clothe you,
O you of little faith? [31]*So do not worry, say-*
ing, 'What shall we eat?' or 'What shall we
drink?' or 'What shall we wear?' [32]*For the*
pagans run after all these things, and your
heavenly Father knows that you need
them. [33]*But seek first his kingdom and his*
righteousness, and all these things will be
given to you as well. [34]*Therefore do not*
worry about tomorrow, for tomorrow will
worry about itself. Each day has enough
trouble of its own.

[a]27 Or *single cubit to his height*

Group Questions

TO BEGIN / 15 Minutes (Choose 1 or 2)

- ❑ When you were a teenager, what did your parents (and their generation) think of your clothes?
- ❑ Who is the "worry wart" in your family?
- ❑ Who is the Rock of Gibraltar in your family—steadfast even in the hardest of times?

READ SCRIPTURE AND DISCUSS / 30 Minutes

- ❑ Since the disciples' focus should be on heavenly treasure and their loyalty to God rather than money (last unit), Jesus moves on to instruct his disciples about the proper attitude toward their material needs. What is the essential point of this passage?
- ❑ What is the opposite of worry (v. 30)? As you get more things, do you worry less—or more?
- ❑ Why does worrying about your needs show a lack of dependence on God? What does the illustration of God's care for the birds and lilies teach you?
- ❑ Are God's children, being "much more valuable" than birds (v. 26), exempt from hunger, famine and other suffering (see note on v. 26)? If you're not promised trouble-free days (v. 34), what *are* you promised?
- ❑ "But seek first his kingdom ... (v. 33)" What does this mean? Get rid of your Porsche? Put God first and keep the Porsche? Check it out with God first? Volkswagen buyers are holier?
- ❑ "Do not worry about tomorrow ... (v. 34)" What is Jesus saying? Don't plan ahead? Plan ahead so you don't worry? Live for today? Take life as it comes? Trust God with things you can't control?
- ❑ Other Scriptures call upon people to plan ahead, work hard, and provide for their families (Pr. 6:6–8; 10:4; 2 Th. 3:6–12). How can you reconcile those admonitions with Jesus' emphasis in the Sermon on the Mount?
- ❑ Why pray when you can worry?! What are the biggest concerns facing you right now—things that are the easiest to worry about and the hardest to pray about with faith? What does it mean for you to seek God's kingdom in the midst of your anxieties?

TO CLOSE AND PRAY / 15-30 Minutes

- ❑ Do Jesus' words in this passage make this study series heavier or lighter for you?
- ❑ How can your brothers and sisters in this group support you and join you in prayer?

Notes

6:25–34 The implication of serving God and not money (v.24) is that the disciple need not worry about the necessities of life (specifically, food, drink, and clothing). By way of illustrating the fact that God takes care of those who follow him, Jesus notes that birds depend upon God for their food, and flowers depend on him for their beautiful adornment. His point is that God's children, who are more valuable than the birds and the flowers, can therefore depend upon God to show the same care for them that he gives to bird and plants. To worry is to show a lack of dependence on God.

6:25 ***Therefore I tell you.*** This passage spells out the significance of the principles Jesus laid down in verses 19–24. Since disciples of Jesus have a heavenly treasure (v. 20), their eye is focused on the good things of God (v. 22), and their loyalty is to God and not Money; *therefore,* they need not be anxious about the material needs of life.

do not worry. Worry or anxiety is a state of mind. Having chosen God's way, the disciple must not be overly concerned about the demands and pressures that occupy those committed to the other way (materialism).

Is not life more important than food?... The materialistic quest reduces life to a matter of keeping the body fed and dressed. While that is a necessary part of life, the materialistic answer makes this the central focus.

6:26 In showing the folly of making concern for food the central focus of life, Jesus points out how God provides for the needs of the birds. The point is not that his disciples need not do anything to feed themselves, but that their ultimate trust rests in God to meet their needs. "What is prohibited is worry, not work" (France).

much more valuable. The point of the creation story (Genesis 1) is to stress God as Creator of all and the role of humanity as God's representative on earth, charged with the responsibility to "rule" the earth (such that it is nurtured and prosperous). It is because humanity has a special relationship and responsibility to the Creator that people are "more valuable" than animals. Since God meets the needs of the animals, will he not do so for people? This does not mean that Christians are somehow exempt from the possibility of hunger or famine. The common sufferings of humanity affect believers, too. The point of the passage is that we are fed, not by our own efforts, but by God's mercy. Hoarding and preoccupation with material concerns reflect a lack of trust in God as the ultimate provider. This is especially the case when one person (or nation) hoards goods at the expense of others. In general, it is not the earth's inability to feed its population that leads to famines, rather it is the human predilection to use food as a political weapon (or as a means of social control) that so often accounts for the mass suffering involved in famines. Those who could help hoard instead of share. The same Jesus who here promises that God feeds the hungry likewise commands his followers to be the agents through which the food is given (25:31–46).

6:27 ***a single hour.*** Jesus' point is that since all the worry in the world cannot even add an hour to one's life, what is the purpose of worrying? (Modern medicine might add that worry actually will probably *reduce* one's life span through stress-related diseases!) While the older versions of the Bible rendered this "a single cubit," this translation makes more sense in this context. Even if worry *could* add a single hour to one's entire life, that would not be a very significant payoff for all the anxiety. However, if worry could actually add a cubit (about 18 inches) to one's height, that would be a major accomplishment!

6:28–30 Following through on his comment in verse 25, Jesus now encourages his followers to consider how even flowers, unable to rush about in anxious pursuit of their physical needs, are adorned with beauty. Since God provides them with such beauty, why should his people fear that they will be neglected by God?

6:29 Solomon. Solomon, the third king of Israel, was noted for his fabulous wealth (1Ki 10:14–29). The folly of being anxious about clothes is revealed in that even the simplest flower is adorned more delicately and attractively than the richest man or woman.

6:30 thrown into the fire. Some of the flowers Jesus has in mind are not the ornamental ones most often noticed for their beauty. Even weeds that were commonly used for fuel have a beauty that far surpasses their intended use. Therefore, people can have the assurance God will not forget to provide them with needed clothes.

you of little faith. This is a single Greek word meaning "little-faiths." Matthew uses it four of the five times it appears in the NT (8:26; 14:31; 16:8; 17:20). As the two illustrations here show, faith is reliance on the love, care, and power of God. Faith is the opposite of anxiety.

6:31 ***So do not worry.*** Again, what is commended here is not idleness but faith. As verse 33 indicates, the disciples of Jesus are to be busy, but their activity is centered around pursuing God's agenda; they are not to be centered around simply meeting their own needs. They are to be confident that God will meet their needs.

What shall we eat/drink/wear?. This is the "world's Trinity of cares" (Stott).

6:33 Having described where their attention is *not* to be directed (toward worry), Jesus now tells his disciples where their focus *is* meant to be: They are to be oriented toward God's unfolding work ("his kingdom") and on acts that reflect his nature ("his righteousness"). All of one's life—from one's inner attitudes to one's social involvements—is to be brought under this overriding purpose. The supreme ambition of the Christian is that all that he or she thinks, says, and does be for the glory of God. The implication of this verse is that if a disciple is focused on finding and doing the will of God, then that disciple will not worry about material things. His or her needs are in the hands of God.

6:34 ***tomorrow.*** Worry generally has to do with the future, about what lies ahead. The disciple is to live one day at a time, and not in dread of what might happen in the future.

trouble. Disciples are not promised a trouble-free life; they are, however, promised God's care.

Notes (Continued)

The Simple Life

Richard Foster defines this commitment to following Jesus as the discipline of *simplicity,* of living for one thing (the kingdom of God) as opposed to the fragmented loyalties of the rest of the world. He writes, "Freedom from anxiety is characterized by three inner attitudes.

- To receive what we have as a gift from God is the first inner attitude of simplicity.
- To know that it is God's business, and not ours to care for what we have is the second inner attitude of simplicity.
- To have our goods available to others marks the third inner attitude of simplicity."

Foster goes on to say that simplicity is not only an inner attitude, it also has an outward expression. The questions below reflect seven of the overall principles Foster suggests we consider as a way of reflecting about how the way we live shows what is really central to us. These are not the only questions that could be asked, but they are helpful ones in applying the idea of simplicity to twentieth-century life.

- Do I buy things for their usefulness rather than for their status? Do I sometimes act as though my happiness is really tied up with owning some certain product ? Do I attempt to stay within my means and avoid financing schemes?

- Am I willing to reject anything that might be producing an addiction in me (i.e., a sense that I could just not do without _______________)?

- Am I able to enjoy things without having to possess them as my own? In what ways am I learning the freedom of giving things away?

- Am I appreciative of the beauty of the creation?

- Are honesty and integrity the distinguishing characteristics of my speech?

- Am I free to reject anything (e.g., possessions or positions) that breeds the oppression of others?

- Do I shun whatever would distract me from my number-one priority—to seek first God's kingdom and righteousness? Do I actively cultivate attitudes and actions that would help me in this pursuit?

(Taken from *Celebration of Discipline,* Richard J. Foster, Harper & Row)

UNIT 11—Judging Others/Ask, Seek, Knock / Matthew 7:1–12

Scripture

Judging Others

***7** Do not judge, or you too will be judged.*
[2]For in the same way you judge others,
you will be judged, and with the measure
you use, it will be measured to you.
[3]"Why do you look at the speck of saw-
dust in your brother's eye and pay no
attention to the plank in your own eye?
[4]How can you say to your brother, 'Let me
take the speck out of your eye,' when all
the time there is a plank in your own eye?
[5]You hypocrite, first take the plank out of
your own eye, and then you will see clear-
ly to remove the speck from your brother's
eye.
[6]"Do not give dogs what is sacred; do not
throw your pearls to pigs. If you do, they
may trample them under their feet, and
then turn and tear you to pieces.

Ask, Seek, Knock

[7]"Ask and it will be given to you; seek
and you will find; knock and the door will
be opened to you. [8]For everyone who asks
receives; he who seeks finds; and to him
who knocks, the door will be opened.
[9]"Which of you, if his son asks for bread,
will give him a stone? [10]Or if he asks for a
fish, will give him a snake? [11]If you, then,
though you are evil, know how to give
good gifts to your children, how much
more will your Father in heaven give good
gifts to those who ask him! [12]So in every-
thing, do to others what you would have
them do to you, for this sums up the Law
and the Prophets.

Group Questions

TO BEGIN / 15 Minutes (Choose 1 or 2)

- ❑ Were your parents too strict or too lenient? What would your children say about you?
- ❑ As a child, how often did you get the gift at the top of your Christmas list? How often do you now?
- ❑ How well do you accept criticism?

READ SCRIPTURE AND DISCUSS / 30 Minutes

- ❑ The "surpassing righteousness" (5:20) of the members of the kingdom does not give them permission to be judgmental toward others. Who will judge them for their condemning judgmentalism (vv. 1–2)?
- ❑ Does Jesus' humorous illustration (vv. 3–5) mean we should never criticize others? Why or why not? What type of inner character is Jesus calling for?
- ❑ Where are you tempted to see others' "specks" and ignore your own "plank"? Home? Work? Church? Small group? What can you do about this?
- ❑ Does v. 6 call for appropriate "judging" (see Note on v. 6)? In situations of significant moral or doctrinal issues, does Jesus call for no judgment? Divine judgment only? Fair judgment? Self judgment first?
- ❑ When it comes to judging, do you tend to be hard on yourself or on others; harder on those you love or harder on those you do not know?
- ❑ What is your response to vv. 7–11? It's about time we got to something positive? I'm ready to ask ... and receive? "Ask, seek, knock"—must be tough to get in? This sounds nice, but it's been a long time since I've gotten any supernatural "good gifts"?
- ❑ Though this section is Jesus' encouragement to come to God in confident prayer continuously (see notes on vv. 7–11), is this a blank check promise regarding prayer? Why or why not? What would God do if you were unknowingly asking for a "stone" or "snake"?
- ❑ How does the "Golden Rule" in v. 12 sum up all that the Law and Prophets are about, as well as provide the climax and summary of the Sermon on the Mount? What slight, yet enormous, change did Jesus make to a previously well-known rule (see note on v. 12)?

TO CLOSE AND PRAY / 15-30 Minutes

- ❑ Has your group kept the Golden Rule—doing to other members what you would have them do to you?
- ❑ What personal concerns do you need to "ask," "seek" and "knock on the door" about today?

Notes

7:1–5 The "surpassing righteousness" of the members of the kingdom (5:20) is not to be license for a judgmental attitude toward others. In typical rabbinic fashion, Jesus lays down the principle (v.1), provides a theological reason for it (v.2), and then illustrates it (vv.3–5).

7:1 ***Do not.*** This is a strong imperative meaning "Stop it!"

judge. In this context, this word refers to a condemning attitude that seeks to pass sentence upon the faults in others. This is not to say that disciples are never to make moral judgments about the actions of others (e.g., 7:15–20 requires them to do so in certain instances); rather, it condemns a harsh and censorious attitude toward others. Such an attitude would betray a lack of the personal brokenness and humility so central to the character of those who pursue God's kingdom (5:3,5).

you will be judged. While the normal human response to criticism is to criticize the one making the judgment, this phrase more likely refers to the fact that such an attitude sets one up to be scrutinized even more carefully by God in the final judgment.

7:2 ***the measure you use.*** This proverbial saying (see Mk 4:24 for its use in an entirely different context) was based on the rabbinic teaching that God would judge the world with two measures, one of justice and one of mercy. If one wished to be dealt with mercifully by God, then that person should deal mercifully with others (cf. 6:14–15).

7:3–5 Jesus uses a vivid, humorous hyperbole (that also has its roots in rabbinic tradition) to express how hypocritical it is to judge the minor fault of another in the light of the enormity of one's own unrecognized sin.

7:4 ***speck.*** The word refers to something very small, like a splinter of wood or a bit of sawdust.

plank. The folly of trying to clear out a speck in another person's eye when one is blinded by a whole piece of wood in one's own is obvious.

7:5 It is not that the other person has no fault. There is a speck there. The problem is that people are more prone to notice the faults of others while they ignore the glaring difficulties and sins in their own lives.

Notes (Continued)

hypocrite. See note on 6:2. The Pharisees are always in the background of the various teachings in this sermon.

7:6 While difficult to interpret, this brief parable (unique to Matthew) may have been intended as a balance to the command in verse 1. While a censorious, condemning attitude has no place in the life of a follower of Jesus, discernment and discrimination are needed. The issue in verses 1-5 is self-righteous judgment of others, not, as required here, a clear-headed sense of where others are in terms of their commitments.

what is sacred. It may be that what is meant here is the flesh of animals offered for sacrifice in the temple services. It would be unthinkable for a priest to carelessly toss such flesh to dogs, who would make no distinction between it and other carrion they might devour.

pearls. Something as precious as pearls would never be given to pigs. Not only would they be unable to appreciate their beauty, but they would trample them underfoot as something useless (since they are not edible). The early church interpreted the sacred food and the pearls as the Eucharist, which it forbade to those who were not baptized. Stott and others suggest that it is better to see the pearls and holy food as metaphors for the good news of the kingdom of God. The disciples are not to continue to share precious spiritual truth with those who are unable or unwilling to see its value. To do so is only to invite blasphemy and abuse. This principle is seen in Jesus' words to the disciples when he sends them out to preach in 10:11–16.

dogs/pigs. The dogs here were wild, violent animals. Pigs were ceremonially unclean animals which Jews would neither eat nor raise (cf. 2Pe 2:22). The type of people in view are those who have deliberately rejected the ways of God.

7:7–11 This section is Jesus' encouragement for his disciples to come to God in prayer continuously, in confidence that God is good and desires to meet their needs.

7:7 ***ask/seek/knock.*** Each of these verbs is a present imperative, which means "keep on asking," "keep on seeking," and "keep on knocking." They should be read as three phrases, each emphasizing the same point ("to ask" is the same as "to seek" which is the same as "to knock"), rather than as a description of increased intensity in prayer.

it will be given/ you will find/ it will be opened. The point of this verse is not that people will only be granted requests from God if they show increasing intensity in prayer (by first asking, then seeking, then knocking and demanding attention!), but to assure the disciples that God will indeed respond to the needs of those who pray.

7:9–11 Once again Jesus uses an analogy to make his point. The way a good father treats his child is how God treats his children.

bread/fish. The most common food in Galilee.

snake. This is probably an eel-like fish without scales that Jews were forbidden to eat (Lev 11:12).

you who are evil. This strong statement is meant to contrast the absolute goodness of God with the sinfulness that stains even the best of human parents. The point is that since usually not even human sinfulness will cause a father to deny food to his own son, how could one think that God would deny any good thing needed by those who call upon him?

7:12 This is the so-called Golden Rule. While it has no immediate connection to the teaching on prayer in verses 7–11, it does sum up what the righteousness of the disciples is to look like. It provides a foundational perspective on all human relationships. The negative form of this rule was widely known in the ancient world: "Do not do to others what you do not want them to do to you." Such diverse figures as Confucius and the great rabbi Hillel taught this. It is also found in Hinduism, Buddhism, as well as in Greek and Roman teaching. Jesus, however, alters this statement in a slight but highly significant way. He shifts this statement from the negative ("Do not") to the positive ("Do"). By so doing, he provided the world with one of the great (and rare) advances in moral understanding. Whereas the negative rule was fulfilled by inaction (not bothering others), the positive rule requires active benevolence (working for the good of others). The law of non-interference has become the law of love.

So. This links the Golden Rule to all the previous teaching in this section. This is the climax and summary of the Sermon on the Mount.

this sums up the Law and the Prophets. The Golden Rule succinctly defines the essence of what the OT teaching about human relationships was meant to accomplish (see also Mk 12:30–31 and Rom 13:8–10).

On Judging . . .

by D. Martyn Lloyd-Jones

"(A judgmental attitude) was something that troubled the early Church; and it has constantly troubled the Church of God ever since.

"What is this danger against which our Lord is warning us? We can say first of all that it is a kind of spirit ... a self-righteous spirit ... a feeling that we are all right while others are not. That then leads to censoriousness, and a spirit that is always ready to express itself in a derogatory manner. And then, accompanying that, there is the tendency to despise others, to regard them with contempt.

"It seems to me, further, that a very vital part of this spirit is the tendency to be hypercritical... which means (someone who) delights in criticism for its own sake and enjoys it...

"It shows itself in a readiness to give judgment when the matter is of no concern to us at all. How much of our time do we spend in expressing our opinion about people who really have no direct dealings with us? ...

"A further way in which we may know whether we are guilty of this is to ask if we habitually express our opinion without a knowledge of all the facts.

"Another indication of it is that it never takes the trouble to understand the circumstances, and it is never ready to excuse; it is never ready to exercise mercy. (Someone) with a charitable spirit ... is prepared to listen and to see if there is an explanation ... to see if there may be mitigating circumstances. But the man who judges says, 'No, I require nothing further.'

"But perhaps we can end the description and bring it to its awful revolting climax by putting it like this: This spirit really manifests itself in the tendency to pronounce final judgment upon people as such ... it is not a judgment so much on what they do, or believe, or say, as upon the persons themselves. It is a final judgment upon an individual, and what makes it so terrible is that at that point it is arrogating to itself something that belongs to God" (*Studies on the Sermon on the Mount, Vol. 2, Eerdmans,* pp. 166–169).

UNIT 12—The Narrow and Wide Gates / Matthew 7:13–23

Scripture

The Narrow and Wide Gates

***13* "Enter through the narrow gate. For**
wide is the gate and broad is the road that
leads to destruction, and many enter
through it. 14But small is the gate and nar-
row the road that leads to life, and only a
few find it.

A Tree and Its Fruit

***15* "Watch out for false prophets. They**
come to you in sheep's clothing, but
inwardly they are ferocious wolves. 16By
their fruit you will recognize them. Do peo-
ple pick grapes from thornbushes, or figs
from thistles? 17Likewise every good tree
bears good fruit, but a bad tree bears bad
fruit. 18A good tree cannot bear bad fruit,
and a bad tree cannot bear good fruit.
19Every tree that does not bear good fruit is
cut down and thrown into the fire. 20Thus,
by their fruit you will recognize them.
21 "Not everyone who says to me, 'Lord,
Lord,' will enter the kingdom of heaven,
but only he who does the will of my Father
who is in heaven. 22Many will say to me on
that day, 'Lord, Lord, did we not prophesy
in your name, and in your name drive out
demons and perform many miracles?'
23Then I will tell them plainly, 'I never knew
you. Away from me, you evildoers!'

Group Questions

TO BEGIN / 15 Minutes (Choose 1 or 2)

- ❑ What is your favorite fruit?
- ❑ When you're lost, do you usually stop and ask for directions, or drive around until you find your way?
- ❑ Are you more likely to trust people until they blow it, or distrust them until they prove themselves?

READ SCRIPTURE AND DISCUSS / 30 Minutes

- ❑ Jesus begins the conclusion to the Sermon contrasting genuine commitment against more formal commitment to his way. Where do the two roads, in vv. 13–14 lead? Which is the road less traveled?
- ❑ Are "destruction" and "life" reserved only for eternity, or do they also depict people's condition now? Why?
- ❑ In the next section (vv. 18–20), who were the "false prophets" in "sheep's clothing" in Jesus' time (see note on v. 15)?
- ❑ Who are the wolves in sheep's clothing today? How can you identify them (see note on v. 16a)?
- ❑ According to vv. 21–23, what is wrong with a mere profession of faith?
- ❑ If prophesying, driving out demons, and performing miracles isn't what Jesus means by doing "the will of my Father" (v. 21), then what *is*? What makes a person eligible to enter the kingdom (see note on v. 22)?
- ❑ Are *you* calling upon Jesus as Lord by acknowledging his sovereignty over your life, looking to him for mercy, and humbly living in accordance with his teachings?

TO CLOSE AND PRAY / 15-30 Minutes

- ❑ Next week will be the last session in this Bible study. Would you like to continue the group after that? Maybe multiply into two groups?
- ❑ This has been a "heavy" course. How can you celebrate this time together? Have a party . . .?
- ❑ If you were to describe the fruitfulness of your spiritual life right now, what would you say: Still in the bud? Growing, but not yet mature? Ripe and juicy? Bruised and wormy? Please explain.
- ❑ How can your group members pray for you?

Notes

7:13–27 The Sermon on the Mount is concluded by another four sets of contrasts (cf. 6:19–34) in which Jesus calls his disciples to genuine commitment over against mere formal commitment to his way. Having taught the way of surpassing righteousness (5:20), these four pictures call Matthew's readers to make a choice. In spite of all the apparent choices and opinions in the world today, these passages remind us that ultimately there are only two alternatives before us. There are only two ways (broad and narrow, 7:13–14), only two kinds of teachers (false and true, 7:15–20), only two kinds of followers (doers and sayers, 7:21–23), and only two kinds of foundations (rock and sand, 7:24–27). The choice in each case is between the way of Christ and the way of the world.

7:13–14 The idea of two ways—the way of wickedness and the way of virtue—was taught by Greek writers (e.g., Hesiod), the Psalmists (Ps 1), and by Jewish prophets (e.g., Jer 21:8).

7:13 ***wide is the gate and broad is the road.*** The wide gate and broad road, which is followed by most people, has been described throughout the Sermon. It is the way of life that stands in contrast to the values taught in the Beatitudes.

destruction. This is where the "natural" way leads. Jesus does not define this destiny, but the word he uses for it makes it clear that it is an awful end. While ultimately such a lifestyle leads to the destruction that is part of the wrath of God against sin (Ro 1:18), it is important to keep in mind that a lifestyle marked by the broad way leads to destruction here and now, in the sense of estranged relationships and inner chaos. The broad way, while well traveled, is not particularly pleasant for those who choose it.

7:14 ***small is the gate and narrow the road.*** The narrower road is the way of life advocated in the Sermon. It is the way of humility, compassion, and justice pursued because one is loyal to Jesus as the Lord (5:3–12). It is the way of reconciliation, love, integrity, generosity, and a love without boundaries (5:21–48). It is the way of inner devotion to God (6:1–18) marked by a whole-hearted commitment to God and his ways (6:19–34). It is the way of mercy toward others (7:1–5), and trust in God's goodness (7:7–11). It is the way of actively seeking the good of others (7:12). This way is entered through a narrow gate which requires us to leave behind the baggage of prejudice, selfish ambition, pride, and other loyalties. This way calls for discipline, training, and faith. Such a decision calls for people to go against the sinful tendencies of the broad way that seem so natural. Therefore, it is chosen by fewer people.

life. The narrow way leads to life in all senses of the word. In this life, the narrow way leads to an inner wholeness marked by meaning and purpose (experienced through the presence of God), and to fulfilling relationships marked by integrity and harmony. It also is the way to eternal life with God, since it reflects the character of what that life entails. Jesus will refer to this destiny in verse 21 as "entering the kingdom of God."

few. When asked whether only a few will be saved, Jesus does not answer directly, but calls the questioner to pursue the narrow road (Lk 13:23,24). Jesus does not deal with theoretical abstractions, but calls upon individuals to make the choice to follow him.

7:15–20 Prophets were people who claimed to speak in the name of God. False prophets, whether motivated by a desire for power and prestige or a desire for money, were a problem in both Judaism and Christianity (see Dt 13:1–5; Je 23:9–40; 2Pe 2:1; 1Jn 4:1–3). Their concern was for themselves, not for the glory of God nor the well-being of those whom they influenced.

7:15 ***Watch out.*** Once again the disciple is called upon to make a judgment about other people. In this case, it is necessary to discern who speaks truthfully and who speaks falsely about religious truth.

sheep's clothing. Prophets (like Elijah and John the Baptist) often wore animal skins (2Ki 1:8; Mt 3:4). People might dress in this fashion and (by doing so) claim to be prophets. Or looking at this another way, false prophets might claim to be sheep (an image used for disciples) or they might pretend to be as harmless as sheep, but their true nature is that of vicious wolves who want to feed off others. While the nature of the "dogs" and "pigs" (7:6) is obvious, these wolves are harder to detect, for their intentions and character are masked by outward appearances. Once again, Jesus probably has the Pharisees in mind here.

7:16a ***By their fruit.*** John Stott suggests three ways that the fruit of a Christian teacher is to be tested to see whether it is good or bad: "The first kind of 'fruit' by which false prophets reveal their true identity is in the realm of character and conduct. . .This being so, whenever we see in a teacher the meekness and gentleness of Christ, his love, patience, kindness, goodness and self-control, we have reason to believe him to be true, not false. On the other hand, whenever these qualities are missing, and 'the works of the flesh' are more apparent than 'the fruit of the Spirit' -especially enmity, impurity, jealousy and self-indulgence—we are justified in suspecting that the prophet is an imposter ... A second 'fruit' is the ... actual teaching ... The apostle John gives us an example of this, for the Asian churches to which he wrote had been invaded by false teachers... He encouraged them to (consider) whether the teachers' message was in accord with the original apostolic instruction, and in particular whether it confessed Jesus as the Christ come in the flesh (1 Jn 2:22–24) ... A third test ... concerns their influence. We have to ask ourselves what effect their teaching has on their followers ... Its gangrenous progress is seen when it upsets peoples' faith (2 Ti 2:18), promotes ungodliness (2 Ti 2:16) and causes bitter divisions (1 Ti 6:4; 2 Ti 2:23)." It is on the basis of tests such as these that the church is to evaluate those who would be its leaders.

7:16b Jesus uses two illustrations to show that conduct demonstrates what is true about a person. False prophets will not produce fruit like grapes and figs that nourish people; instead they produce only thorns and thistles which cut and hurt.

7:21–23a Matthew continues to press home the meaning of discipleship by stressing the point that merely saying "Jesus is Lord" is not enough. Such an affirmation is shown to be genuine or false by what a person does. Actions demonstrate the reality of affirmations. Thus, on the Day of Judgment, the false prophets (and others) may protest that they ministered in Jesus' name, but the truth that they never knew him will be revealed.

7:21 ***"Lord, Lord,"*** Such people claim allegiance to Jesus. The earliest Christian confession was "Jesus is Lord" (1Co 12:3), but the fact is that those who do not do his will render this confession meaningless. Luke 6:46 expresses the same point even more succinctly: "Why do you call me 'Lord, Lord' and not do what I tell you to do?"

Notes (Continued)

7:22 *on that day.* This is the Day of Judgment. Throughout the Bible, there is a clear expectation of a final accounting of humanity by God.

Lord, Lord, did we not. Two important aspects of discipleship are accentuated in this sentence: **(1)** Neither verbal allegiance to Jesus, nor powerful actions, nor success in ministry, nor the use of a certain type of "God-talk" can by itself be taken as evidence of a person being a true spokesperson for God. What really counts is whether that person is walking in the ways of God. **(2)** No one will enter the kingdom who attempts to do so on the basis of his or her deeds. These people tried to persuade the Lord to allow them access to his kingdom. The proper way to call upon Jesus as Lord is to acknowledge his sovereignty over all of one's life, look to him for mercy, and humbly live in accordance with his teachings.
A *Calvin and Hobbes* comic strip (10/18/90) caught the meaning of Jesus' comments here about the tree and its fruit:

First panel:

Calvin asks Hobbes: "Do you think people ought to be judged based on their actions, or on the attitudes in their hearts?"

Second panel:

Hobbes replies: "I think what we do reveals what's in our hearts."

Third panel:

Calvin scowls.

Fourth panel:

Calvin yells at Hobbes: "I resent that!"

UNIT 13—The Wise and Foolish Builders / Matt. 7:24–29

Scripture

The Wise and Foolish Builders

24 ***"Therefore everyone who hears these
words of mine and puts them into practice
is like a wise man who built his house on
the rock.*** 25 ***The rain came down, the
streams rose, and the winds blew and beat
against that house; yet it did not fall,
because it had its foundation on the rock.***
26 ***But everyone who hears these words of
mine and does not put them into practice
is like a foolish man who built his house
on sand.*** 27 ***The rain came down, the
streams rose, and the winds blew and beat
against that house, and it fell with a great
crash."***
28 ***When Jesus had finished saying these
things, the crowds were amazed at his
teaching,*** 29 ***because he taught as one who
had authority, and not as their teachers of
the law.***

Group Questions

TO BEGIN / 15 Minutes (Choose 1 or 2)

❑ As a child, were you afraid of storms? When?
❑ If you could build your dream house, where would you build it and what would it be like?
❑ Who is the "wisest" member of your family?

READ SCRIPTURE AND DISCUSS / 30 Minutes

❑ The Sermon concludes with a parable presenting Jesus' listeners with life's ultimate decision (vv. 24–27). What two choices do we have?
❑ What are the similarities and the differences between the two house builders?
❑ How does a person build on the rock? (See "Building Your House Upon A Rock" at end of notes.)
❑ What does the storm represent? Are believers sheltered from life's difficulties? From "collapse"?
❑ Jesus ends his sermon with the picture of the foolish man's house falling with a great crash. Why would Jesus end with a warning and call for repentance?
❑ What percentage of your friends from your early spiritual journey have survived the test of time and "storms"? What storm do you think claims the most casualties: Intellectual doubts? Moral failures? Relational break-ups? Creeping apathy?
❑ The crowds are mentioned again at the end of the Sermon (vv. 28–29). Why were they amazed (see Note on v. 28)?
❑ The final effect of the Sermon on the Mount is to call attention to the one who gave the message. The real question each of us is left with is, "How will you respond to this Jesus?" Well ... ?!

TO CLOSE AND PRAY / 15-30 Minutes

❑ What has been the high point for you in this study? What was the "serendipity"—the unexpected blessing?
❑ If you have decided to continue as a group, what do you appreciate and what would you like to see improved? Who can you invite to join the group?
❑ If you have decided to terminate, what will you miss?
❑ To be a "wise builder" at this point in your life, do you need to learn more or practice what you have already learned?
❑ What "storm" are you going through right now? Do you think you're at the beginning, middle or end? How can the group pray for you in the days ahead?

Notes

7:24–27 Both Matthew's and Luke's version of this Sermon conclude with this parable, which dramatically highlights the choice with which Jesus confronts his listeners. One must decide either to put his teaching into practice or else face the destruction that is the end result of any other choice. People in our culture do not like to be faced with such stark alternatives, especially in the area of religious belief. Jesus, however, clearly teaches that there is only one way of living that leads to life. He himself is the way, the truth, and the life (Jn 14:6), and commitment to him and his teachings is the only way one can survive the judgment of God. All other choices lead to death. The two houses in this parable may look alike (the issue throughout verses 13–27 is the contrast between outward appearance and inner reality), but only the one built on a solid foundation (obedience to God) will stand when the storm (of God's ultimate accounting) comes.

7:24 ***Therefore.*** The parable concludes the argument presented in verses 13–23. The choices one makes about the path one travels (vv.13–14), who one listens to (vv.15–20), and how one lives (vv.21–23) all boil down to the ultimate choice of whether or not a person will build his or her life upon the foundation of Jesus and his teachings.

like a wise man. In the OT, the wise person is the one who chooses to center his or her life around the truth of God's character and Law (Ps 111:10, Pr 3:5–7; 9:10). In contrast, the fool is the person who (regardless of how intelligent he or she may be) assumes that there is no ultimate consequence of living life in disregard to God and the Law (Ps 14:1; Pr 14:16). In this parable, both kinds of people hear Jesus' words.The difference in their character is shown in how they respond to his teachings. "Both men ... are builders, for to live means to build. Every ambition a man cherishes, every thought he conceives, every word he speaks, and every deed he performs is, as it were, a building block. Gradually the structure of his life rises" (Hendriksen).

on the rock. Houses whose foundations were secured to bedrock would be able to survive a bad storm. In this context, the rock is Jesus and his teaching.

7:25 Palestine was dry most of the year. But in the autumn, rains came and flash floods swept down the ravines. What looks like a fine place to build a house

Notes (Continued)

in the dry season may become a raging torrent during flood season.

7:26 ***on sand.*** Building on sand is easier; if there is no settling of the land, nor any pressure of wind or water, the house will stand just fine.

7:27 ***the rain came, the streams rose, and the winds blew.*** Ultimately, the image of a storm is used as a picture of God's coming judgment upon the world (Hab 3:9–12). The Bible as a whole, as well as Jesus' teachings in particular, speaks clearly of God's judgment. It is in light of the inevitability of God's judgment that people are urged to repent and look to Christ as the one who will deliver them from this judgment. However, the rains and wind do not only represent the final judgment. They also represent the hardships in this life that fall upon both believers and non-believers. Believers are not promised that they will be sheltered from life's difficulties, but that they can have a foundation that will allow them to stand through such troubles.

it fell. There is no hope for a house built on sand when the flood waters erode away the very basis upon which it stands. Those whose life is built upon pride, power, or possessions have no hope when confronted with realities that wipe these things away.

with a great crash. The fall of the house, a symbol of the person who lives apart from God's ways, is graphically presented. Such will be the fate of those who ignore the message contained within this Sermon. Matthew ends the Sermon with this stark warning and its implicit call to repent.

7:28–29 The crowds, present at the beginning of the Sermon (5:1–2), are again brought into the picture.

7:28 ***When Jesus had finished saying these things.*** This is Matthew's way of signaling the close of a major section of Jesus' teaching in order to make a transition to a new part of his narrative (see 11:1; 13:53; 19:1; 26:1).

amazed. The reaction of the crowds stresses the radically new message Jesus brought. He had shown that the kingdom belonged not to the Jews who would fight the Romans, but to all people who humbled themselves before God. He had shown that the Law, which Judaism prized (as what set them apart from everyone else) really condemned them, since even their most zealous members (the Pharisees) had failed to embrace its teachings. He had pointed out a new way of living that called for a deep inner integrity, humility, graciousness, and love. He repudiated the religious system for being concerned only with externals. He said there was no reward from God for that type of behavior. He forced people to seriously consider what truly motivated them. He stressed the need for a conscious decision to choose God's ways. All of this would cause his listeners to wonder who was delivering such a new, radical call requiring absolute allegiance to himself. The final effect of the Sermon on the Mount is to call attention to the one who gave this message. The real question Matthew leaves the reader with is, "How will I respond to this Jesus?"

7:29 ***their teachers of the law.*** Literally, "scribes," religious lawyers who interpreted Jewish law. Originally, it was their job to make copies of the OT. Because of their familiarity with Scripture, people consulted them about points of law, and hence their role evolved into that of teacher of the law. Their authority rested in their ability to quote the writings of earlier rabbis to prove their points. In contrast, Jesus' power lay in his message's implicit moral force and in the fact that he called upon no outside authority to validate his teaching.

Building Your House Upon a Rock

by D. Martyn Lloyd-Jones

[The person who builds his or her house on the rock is the one who:]

"... allows every part of the Bible to speak to him ... he does not rush to a few favorite Psalms and use them as a kind of hypnotic when he cannot sleep at night; he allows the whole Word to examine him and search him ... In other words, the true Christian humbles himself under the Word ... the man who is right with respect to this Sermon is a man who, having humbled himself, submits himself to it, becomes poor in spirit, becomes a mourner for his sins, becomes meek because he knows how worthless he is. He immediately conforms to the Beatitudes because of the effect of the Word upon him, and then, because of that, he desires to conform to the type and pattern set before him ... Any man who desires to live this type and kind of life is a Christian. He hungers and thirsts after righteousness; that is the big thing in his life ... Observe the nature of the test. It is not asking whether you are sinless or perfect; it is asking what you would like to be, what you desire to be.

"... the true believer ... (is one whose) supreme desire is to do these things (in the Sermon) and be like the Lord Jesus Christ. It means he is a man who not only wants forgiveness, not only wants to escape hell and go to heaven. Quite as much, he wants positive holiness in this life and in this world ... That is the man who builds upon the rock. He is a man who desires and prays for holiness and who strives after it. He does his utmost to be holy, because his supreme desire is to know Christ ... to know Christ now, to have Christ as his Brother, to have Christ as his Companion, to be walking with Christ in the light now, to enjoy a foretaste of heaven here in this world of time—that is the man who builds upon the rock. He is a man who loves God for God's sake, and whose supreme desire and concern is that God's name and God's glory may be magnified and spread abroad.

"That is what is meant by practicing the Sermon on the Mount. If, on the other hand, you find that you cannot answer these tests satisfactorily, there is but one inevitable conclusion: you have been building upon the sand. And your house will collapse ... You will see, then, that you have nothing. If you see that now, admit it, confess it to God without a second's delay. Confess it and humble yourself 'under the mighty hand of God.' Acknowledge it and cast yourself upon His love and mercy, tell Him that, at last, you desire to be holy and righteous; ask Him to give you His Spirit and to reveal to you the perfect work of Christ on your behalf. Follow Christ, and He will lead you to this true holiness, 'without which no man shall see the Lord' " (*Studies in the Sermon on the Mount*, Vol. 2, Eerdmans, pp.312–314).

ACKNOWLEDGEMENTS

It is not possible (nor desirable) to tackle as formidable a subject as the Sermon on the Mount without the aid of others. The standard exegetical tools have, of course, been used: The Arndt and Gingrich *Greek-English Lexicon of the New Testament; The Interpreter's Dictionary of the Bible, etc.* In addition, reference has been made to a series of fine commentaries: Albright, W. F., and Mann, C.S., *Matthew, The Anchor Bible,* Doubleday, Garden City, NY, 1971. Betz, Hans Dieter, *Essays on the Sermon on the Mount,* Fortress Press, Philadelphia, PA, 1985. Bonhoeffer, Dietrich, *The Cost of Discipleship,* MacMillan Publishing Company, New York, NY, 1963. Bruce, F.F.,*The Hard Sayings of Jesus,* InterVarsity Press, Downers Grove, IL, 1983. France, R.T. *Matthew,* Tyndale New Testament Commentaries, Eerdmans, Grand Rapids, MI, 1985. Hendriksen, William, *The Gospel of Matthew,* Baker Book House, Grand Rapids, MI, 1973. Hill David, *The Gospel of Matthew: The New Century Bible Commentary,* Eerdmans, Grand Rapids, MI. 1981. Kepler, Thomas (ed.), *The Fellowship of the Saints,* Abingdon Press, New York, NY, 1948. Lapide, Pinchas, *The Sermon on the Mount,* Orbis Books, Maryknoll, NY, 1986. Lloyd-Jones, D. Martin, *Studies in the Sermon on the Mount,* Eerdmans, Grand Rapids, MI, 1960. Mounce, Robert H., *Matthew: A Good News Commentary,* Harper and Row, San Francisco, CA 1985. Patte, Daniel, *The Gospel According to Matthew,* Fortress Press, Philadelphia, PA 1987. Stott, John R.W., *Christian Counter-Culture,* InterVarsity Press, Downers Grove, IL, 1978. Vaught, Carl G., *The Sermon on the Mount: A Theological Interpretation,* State University of New York Press, Albany, NY, 1986.

Copyright Endorsements